Reaching Out

Written and illustrated by:

Matilda Lee

About the cover:
Little Tillie found delight in picking mushrooms. They pop up so quickly. As Tillie grew, she found that life changes also pop up quickly.

DEDICATION

There were many good things and many hard things in my life. Through it all, God has kept me lovingly, safe and secure in the palm of His hand. I choose to think on the good things.

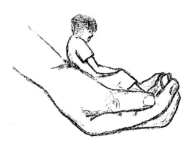

"As he thinketh in his heart, so is he."
Proverbs 23:7
"... I will uphold thee with the right hand of my righteousness." Isaiah 41:10 b
I dedicate this book to my children, grandchildren, great-grandchildren, and those to come.

ACKNOWLEDGMENTS

I thank those who helped me with this project. A special thanks to Rueben and Lena King for urging me to. I thank Lydia (Rene) Kegerreis for editing this book. I also thank Paul Yoder for formatting, editing, and publishing the second edition.

These, my memories, were written in the 1990s and are not to be copied without permission except by family and relatives for use by family and relatives.

CONTENTS

1 PRESCHOOL YEARS

My Arrival into My Family

I arrived on Halloween night, 1927, in a Dover, Delaware farmhouse to Daniel and Katie Byler Lee. I was named Matilda Lee but quickly came to be called Tillie. I had a fair complexion, dark brown eyes and red hair, quite a contrast to my parents who both had black hair.

My mother's hair was curly and black as ink. Her long hair was drawn into a bun at the back of her head but spirals of ringlets would escape at the temple. More ringlets could be seen dangling at the back of her neck. Her brown eyes danced and sparkled when her laughter rang out like clear ringing bells. My

grandfather Byler told me that because he enjoyed her sweet laughter and zest for life, he really missed Mom when, at age 19, she married my dad.

Mom, at five feet, one inch, and just a little bit plump, was much shorter than my dad. Dad was almost six feet tall. His hair was black, but not as ink black as Mom's. He was handsome, with a fair complexion, delightfully friendly, kind and polite. He enjoyed fun.

I can imagine the love and contentment I felt as Mom held me in her arms with Dad coming close to see me. Their familiar soft voices were comforting.

I can imagine Lydia's wonderment the next morning, as my parents showed Lydia her new baby sister. At one year and five days old, Lydia was hardly old enough to comprehend it all.

Lydia had black curly hair and brown eyes. We soon grew to be playmates. Our sister Bertha was born a year after me and we grew up as a threesome. After Bertha arrived and Dad told Grandpa Bylers the news, Grandpa said, "Hurrah for the girls of Delaware."

Down through the years eight more children were born into the family. Their names, according to age, are as follows: Albert, Edwin, John, Henry, Gideon, Lena, Betty, and

Simon. All had curly hair except Edwin, Simon, and myself. As a small boy, Edwin had reddish brown hair. Dad had a reddish beard, but only I had red hair. Until my teen years I did not know anyone with red hair.

We were a happy family. I never heard my parents quarrel. They were firm with us and strict, but fair. Together they made decisions for us very carefully and wisely. Once decided upon, that was final. We understood that. We were not allowed to complain, even if we were disappointed. As we grew older we were allowed to appeal our case. If they thought it merited reconsideration, they did and sometimes we were granted our wish.

My parents were both gentle and kind. They were open and honest with us. We knew we were loved. I am grateful to have been born into a family such as mine.

Our House

Our kitchen was very large and had no "modern conveniences". The table was at one end with the wood cook stove at the other end. If you faced the stove, the dry sink was to the left and to the right was a wash stand with a bucket of water, a large dipper and a basin to wash our hands and faces. When we wanted hot water, we heated it on the stove.

Our wooden pump was painted green and was on the porch. We pumped our water 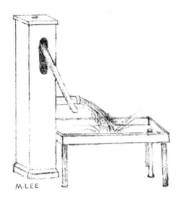 from deep down in the ground. It was good, cold, fresh water. The pump handle was long and could pump water faster than a short handle. A long, wooden, trough-like sink, also painted green, with most of the paint worn off, was built under the pump spout, low to the ground. We set a bucket in that sink, under the spout to catch the water as we pumped. When our feet got dirty we stood in the sink and pumped water on our feet and legs. One of us pumped while the other washed feet. It was a simple, happy and contented life.

One Sunday afternoon my Dad and uncle gathered with us on the porch. They tried to make ice cream with a tin can, using snow to freeze it. They forgot to add salt to the snow so it didn't freeze well.

Dad's Little Girl

Aunt Mollie said I was a timid girl from the first. I still am timid. I don't like being timid. Aunt Mollie also said I was "Dad's little girl." She may be right because some of my earliest memories were when I was out with him picking mushrooms in the orchard early in the dewy morning. I was probably about three years old but I can still feel the awesome effect of the sun shining through the misty, dewy morning. I can feel the excitement of finding mushrooms and the contentment of being with Dad in the early morning quietness and beauty. This was followed by the delicious breakfast of Mom's fried mushrooms and eggs. Another memory is riding with Dad on his dearborn (a horse drawn wagon with side racks, used as a pick-up would be used today.) Dad drove the dearborn between the rows in the grape vineyard to pick up the baskets of grapes the pickers filled. I sat on the seat beside him as he drove from one row to the next. Between the rows he jumped to the ground and called his "getti-ups" to the horse as he gathered the baskets and I sat alone on the seat. The horse would look around as if to see how Dad was getting along, as if to ask, "Is it about time to move along again?"

Dad answered my questions, such as, "What will they do with the grapes where you take them to sell?" We talked about the butterfly I had just seen. We discussed the characteristics of the horse and his constant swatting at the flies with his tail.

In the evenings Dad would play with us. Sometimes he would play scary games, chasing us and snapping like a dog or another animal until we got trapped in a corner. We'd scream in fright but we enjoyed it.

Dad loved to tease. He would lead us on about something that was unrealistic, enjoying our astonishment and uncertainty until he would reveal that he was just joking.

We also enjoyed tussling with Dad. We were three little girls before any boys came along. Dad would hold one of us fast while the other two would try to free her. Or we would all three try to hold him down. He would pretend we could win. We thought, *We've certainly got him down tight*, but somehow, he always managed to free himself. Oh, it was a great time of laughter and glee.

Some winter nights Dad would sit and crack walnuts for us to eat and for Mom to bake a cake. There was so much talk and laughter going on that nut cracking was a lot of fun. Dad had a way of bringing Mom into our fun with his bantering back and forth from us to her and back again. Mom's comments and clear ringing laughter were a pleasure. My oldest sister, Lydia, was usually the life of the party and kept the fun talk and laughter going strong. I wasn't as talkative as she, but enjoyed it all and laughed along with them.

One Sunday dinner I watched in fascination as Dad put cooked potatoes through a potato ricer. It was amazing how the potatoes squeezed out through the tiny holes in long, thin strips and landed so lightly in the dish. They mustn't be stirred but left fluffy. A few dabs of butter on top made them delicious.

Dad was always Mom's willing helper. He made helping fun. He had a tender way of caressing her by running his hand softly across her shoulder whenever he came up to her wherever she stood working. He would tweak her ear and tease her about one thing or another. Once he took her on his lap and rocked her while singing a lullaby. The whole time she struggled to get off while her laughter rang out. I know Dad did it for the entertainment of us girls. We stood around laughing and cheering. At the same time, I was glad when she finally won and got away.

Watching Mom and Dad at Work

Dad had a way of making his chores a pleasure, so we enjoyed being with him. One chore was clipping our fingernails on Sunday mornings. Another was milking. I liked going to the barn with him.

The milk hit the empty bucket hard and fast in a sharp singsong manner, changing to a clunky sound as the bucket filled. As the stream hit the milk already in the bucket it produced foam. As the foam built up the sound became soft and muffled.

When the milking was finished Dad let the cows out to pasture and took the milk into the house where there was a small room off the porch that was for the care of milk.

First Dad poured the milk in the bowl on top of the separator. The bucket he poured from had a wide spout with a strainer to strain out any dirt that may be in the milk. Inside the separator was a bowl that collected any dirt that may have escaped the bucket's strainer. The separator had cone disks to separate the cream from the milk and two long spouts. A bucket sat on a round shelf below one spout to catch the milk as it came out. A crock was set on a round shelf under the other spout to catch the cream.

All three of us girls had a tin cup in the milk room that we held under the milk spout to catch ourselves a nice warm drink of milk. As we got bigger, Dad would sometimes allow us to try to crank the separator after he had it cranked into a rhythm. We were not fast enough to keep up the speed and rhythm so Dad would have to take it again. At the right speed, it had a high pitch whirring sound. If you lose that speed you have to close the milk flow valves because it cannot separate the cream from the milk at a low speed. Dad always listened for that whir before he opened the flow valve to allow the milk through.

Mom would use what she needed of the skim milk for cooking and cottage cheese. She made cottage cheese to sell. Dad fed whey and any skim milk we couldn't use to the pigs. This helped the pigs grow big and fat.

Mom made butter with the cream. She had a tumble butter churn. We took our turns at turning the handle. Around and around went the churn, plopping and swishing the cream until it was butter. The fat part of the cream made the butter. The butter was lifted from the liquid part of the cream. The liquid part is the buttermilk. Mom used what we needed of the buttermilk and sold what she could. The rest of the buttermilk was fed to the pigs. Mom had sales for all the butter we did not need for ourselves. It was a lot of butter.

Children's Work and Play

As we grew older we were asked to help with simple chores. Drying dishes for Mom was not so much fun. I liked carrying wood for the kitchen better. Dad split the kitchen wood into small pieces. It was not too much for me to carry five or six pieces of those. When it was very cold Dad carried the wood.

One time when I carried wood I got sawdust into one eye. It hurt badly and Mom could not get it out. Before I went to bed she made a poultice and tied it over my eye with my eye shut. The next morning my eye did not hurt. The poultice drew out the sawdust.

Another task for us was picking up potatoes. It was fun to see the potatoes pop out of the ground as Dad dug them. After a while we got tired and it wasn't so much fun anymore but we needed to stick to our job.

One morning Mom sent us out to pick a lot of dandelion flowers to make wine for medicine. She put them in crocks to brew. It did not taste good but was a good medicine. Dandelion wine was taken for colds or shock. It was also good to put on cuts and infected wounds. It took a lot of dandelions to make a little wine. It was fun to pick the flowers. I still think dandelions are a pretty flower but realize they are considered a pest.

We loved playing outdoors. I think in the summer we were outside more than in the house. We loved going out after the rain to slosh around in the water puddles. We couldn't always wait until it finished raining and ran out at the tail end of the rain.

Once Dad ran out in a torrent of rain where the water came rushing off the roof like a great spout. I could see that he enjoyed it but I wasn't too sure about trying it myself. Afterward Dad dried himself and changed his clothes but his hair was still soaking wet and plastered down on his head.

One day we girls were playing out by the fence. I got hold of a weed stalk. A bumblebee was on it and stung my thumb. Another time a bumblebee stung me on my forehead. My eye was swollen almost shut.

When I was four, just before Christmas, we three sisters knew Mom had hidden our Christmas gifts in an upstairs closet. We were told not to "peek". My younger sister Bertha and I did peek. When Christmas morning came, without realizing, we talked about our gifts in a way that told on ourselves. To punish our disobedience, we were not allowed to play with our gift the rest of the day. We were allowed to hold our gift a little while before it was put away for the day.

The gifts we had that year were little suitcases. Bertha's and mine were red with black polka dots. Lydia's was blue with black dots. I liked the red better and was glad mine was red. The suitcases were about eight by nine by three inches. Mine is a bit dilapidated but I still keep it.

M·LEE

My grandmother Lee gave each of us sisters a rag doll she made herself. The dolls came complete with dress, coat, and bonnet. The feet were made of black material to be their shoes. Their faces wore out so the faces were replaced once. I colored eyes, nose and mouth on mine when I was ten. After that I don't know what happened to mine or any of them.

Our dog, Nellie was a quiet dog. She was white with brown markings One day a stray dog came along that had rabies. We did not know if the rabid dog bit Nellie or not. We had to pen Nellie up until we knew she wouldn't be getting rabies. It caused quite an excitement until the rabid dog was caught. Dad had a hired boy who took a stick for the dog to bite on and walked the dog to where we could lock him into a pen. Then we had to have a veterinarian check him.

I remember a baby swing that was made from canvas and a wire frame that opened to make a bed or fold to a seat with a table in front to hold toys. It was hung on a hook from the ceiling. There was a spring from the hook to the swing straps so that when a child was in a sitting position he could jump when lowered enough for his feet to touch the floor. When a bed, the swing was drawn up three or four feet off the floor. It was usually in the kitchen where Mom worked.

When I was old enough I took my turn to swing the baby when he cried. That quieted him and often he went to sleep.

Extended Family

The summer I was three my great grandparents from Indiana came to visit Grandpa Bylers and all of us. This was Grandma Byler's parents, Phineas and Catherine Yoder. The only thing I can remember is standing at the window watching them come down the road to our house in the horse drawn buggy. Great Grandpa's hair and long beard showed up snowy white inside the darkness of the buggy.

When I was three years old my grandmother Lee made my sister Lydia and myself each a warm winter dress and a coat. My dress was green with blue glass buttons. Lydia's was red with gold glass buttons. She made the dresses big enough and with enough tucks in the skirt and sleeves to be let out as we grew. That way we could wear them two or three winters. She made mine green to be pretty with my red hair and Lydia's red to be pretty with her black hair. We liked out pretty dresses and felt so dressed up.

One day Lydia came in from play and hung her new coat to dry on the damper of the stovepipe in the living room. To Lydia's dismay the coat caught on fire. Mom came running, grabbed the coat and doused it into a washbasin of water. The fire had burned a big hole in the coat and into the sleeve. It took a lot of repairing.

I had a wart on my left thumb when I was four. That summer Dad's uncle from PA came to see us. He saw the wart and asked me to come to him. He wanted to help my wart. I was afraid he would cut it off and I didn't come close. He kept begging me to come and finally got up to get me. I ran out the door and ran to the other side of the house. When I came around the corner I saw him come around the opposite corner. I ran back the way I came, took a short-cut into another door, ran into the kitchen and hid in the bottom cupboard behind the kitchen cook stove where we kept wood for the stove. He did not see me go in. I stayed in there until they left a little later.

Another day Dad's aunt was with us. When she was ready to leave, she took a bag of candy corn and scattered the candy across the floor. She called, "chick, chick, chick," as if to call the chickens to come get their corn. We knew she meant us. We scrambled as fast as we could to pick up the most candy. Since then I especially like candy corn.

Grandpa Lees lived just a little way up the road from our house. We often walked up to their house on errands or just to "stay a little while." Very few cars were on the road and did not travel fast. My Aunt Barbara, Dad's sister, still lived at home with Grandpas. She was of fair complexion, with dark eyes and black hair. Her hands and fingers were long and slender. I'm told she had a pleasant personality. She died of diphtheria when I was four. At the funeral, no one could go inside to view her. She was placed inside the window and people passed by the window to view her.

I was very sick with pneumonia and could not go to the funeral. I remember hot packs on my chest and being frightened by a dog lying on my bed behind me. I must have cried because suddenly Dad was there, trying to convince me there was no dog. My high fever made me think there was a dog. Although I finally believed him, I was still scared.

On the morning of the funeral Grandmother Byler came to stay with me while the rest of the family was away. She pushed my bed close to the heating stove and gave me a bath. I asked why she is giving my bath instead of my mother and where the others are. I don't remember what answers she gave me, but I was told later that since I was so sick, they didn't want to tell me that Aunt Barbara died. They were afraid that I would worry about dying myself.

When I was four, Aunt Mollie and Uncle Amos married and moved into two of our upstairs rooms. They had their first baby while living in our upstairs. They named her Lydia Irene. I was five when she was born. Since we were not quite over the whooping cough, we were not allowed to go upstairs to see her for a few weeks. When Lydia Irene was a little older, I remember watching Aunt Mollie feeding her applesauce. I was amazed that such a little baby could eat.

In his spare time, Uncle Amos was working on building a little house about a mile away. When the house was finished and they moved in, we still felt closer to them than any other aunt and uncle. Not only did we have the memories of them living with us, but also because they usually lived closer to us than the others.

2 GROWING UP YEARS

Rose Valley School

I was almost six when I started walking more than a mile to school. I walked with my sister Lydia and two neighbor boys. I was excited with this new experience.

Mrs. Massey was the teacher in this one room school for grades one to six. We spoke Pennsylvania Dutch at home and could speak little English. Pennsylvania Dutch is a dialect from one of Germany's provinces.

When some Amish emigrated from Germany to Pennsylvania, they kept the dialect and it began to be called Pennsylvania Dutch. Mrs. Massey was good at teaching the little Amish first graders their English. In the process, she learned to understand a little Pennsylvania Dutch. This helped us to communicate. About half the pupils were Amish children.

One day the Red Cross came to give a lecture on their work and purpose. They gave each of us a Red Cross pin. Later that day, the teacher played records on the Victrola. I was fascinated as the record went around and around, the needle following along the grooves. I couldn't understand how the smooth circles could keep moving towards the center and never come off.

After music class, I could not forget the record. I don't know why I needed to do it, but I took my Red Cross pin and scratched an imaginary record on my desktop. Around and around I went. Suddenly there was a slap on my cheek and the teacher was scolding me. I was horrified and humiliated. I did not cry but tears stung inside my eyelids. I never did anything so dreadful again.

Lessons were hard for me. I had a real problem with reading, but I managed to pass to the second grade.

The Depression/Losing the Farm

Soon after I started school, Dad had to sell the farm and all that he owned. Because of the Great Depression, people had no money to buy his fruit and produce. This meant he could not make the payments on the farm.

One day Dad hired a truck to take a load of peaches a two-hour drive to Pennsylvania. He thought maybe they would sell in Pennsylvania, but the people there didn't have money to buy either. The fruit was just rotting away, so Dad allowed people in our neighborhood to come and get fruit. It was better to give it away than to let it rot and be wasted.

It was sad for my parents to lose all they had. Mom cried and cried. Dad tried to comfort her. I remember how tenderly and softly he talked to her. He looked sad too.

My parents could not have the money from the sale. The money had to go to the bank because of the farm debt. Family members and friends bought one of the cows and some furniture and gave them back to my parents as a gift. They also bought and returned our horse and buggy. This way we had something to travel with, a cow for milk, and some furniture for the next house we moved into. In the spring, when chickens could run outside and find food, Uncle Amos Zook went around the neighborhood among Amish friends and collected donations of chickens to give to my parents. Some gave one chicken; some gave two or three. Times were hard for everyone but people were willing to share with my parents to help them get started again.

We moved to a much smaller house. We didn't have all the land to roam on and have fun like we had on our farm. Now Dad had to work away, on a nearby farm. Dad came home late, at 7 p.m. He was tired when he came but we were all so happy to have him home and be together again.

When we moved off the farm we walked a mile to our teacher's house and rode to school with her. Some boys in the neighborhood rode with her too. Mrs. Massey's car was old. It had a top that would fold down. When it rained we had to stop and let the canvas sides down. When it was sunny, we rolled them up. There was no glass in the windows. In 1935 or 1936 she bought a new car and it had glass windows.

One day during school it rained. On our way home the car slid into the ditch. The tires were quite narrow and slid easily when the sandy road was wet. Back then sand was hauled onto roads to fill in potholes instead of gravel. Cars were also lighter weight. The boys lifted the back end, then the front end and set the car out of the ditch.

At home we made Easter eggs and rolled them down a steep hill in the field behind the house. This was great fun. We enjoyed egg hunts too.

In the summer we played a lot outdoors. One day three-year-old Albert, our brother, came into the house and peeked around the door to the living room, making big eyes. His face was black and streaked from his black, dirty fingers. He looked so funny. Mom and we girls laughed and laughed. I don't know where he got all that black.

That summer Dad came into the barn on the farm where he worked. He heard a ruckus in the bull's pen. Quickly he ran to see and found the bull had his boss butted into a corner. Dad grabbed the hay fork and stuck the bull with the prongs so that the bull's attention was taken away from the boss and the boss freed himself.

One day Uncle Adam Byler came to see us. We girls were out feeding the chickens. While Uncle Adam was talking with us he saw a hand saw among the tools in the buggy shed. He picked it up, held the handle and tucked the other end between his knees. With a stick he tapped out a tune as he bent the saw into a bow. He bent it back and forth, varying the degree of bow to produce different notes. We were fascinated with his tune. We hurried to the kitchen to tell Mom about the wonderful music. Mom came out to see and hear. She was happy about Uncle Adam's skill.

Mom made steamed bread. We called it "dompf gnepp." Mom would take a little of the bread dough, roll it into a ball, and lay it on a plate. When it had risen she set the plate on a rack in a large cooking pot with water in the bottom of it and steamed the bread about an hour. It is important to eat it as soon as it is done because it is better that way. We broke off pieces to serve, as it would not do to cut it. We put fruit over it in our bowls and added milk to it. It was delicious.

Spending the Night with the Neighbors

We had neighbors with two teen-age children. We were fond of this family. The father was lively, funny and a big talker. He was short and stocky. When he laughed, he laughed heartily. His wife was tall and heavy. She was motherly with a kind and generous spirit. I don't remember the daughter as well as I do the son, Toby, who played with us. He was the younger of the two children, perhaps 13 years old. Once when we visited there was snow and he took us sledding. He had long legs and could take us fast! We walked past their house on our way to school and back. I always watched to see if he was outdoors because he would be sure to call out to us good-naturedly.

In the summer, we girls were told we could spend the night with those neighbors. It seems strange that I don't remember much about my visit there, other than being tucked in bed by the mother and asking rather persistently the next morning if it wasn't time for my Dad to be coming for us.

Dad finally came for us after lunch. I was so glad to see him. It seemed I had been gone from home so long. Dad was happy and he had news for us! "We have a new baby," he said. "He is a boy and his name is Henry." We could hardly wait to see him. When we went in to see Henry, Dad said we needed to be quiet because Mom wasn't feeling well and was tired. She was lying in bed. I did not like having Mom sick and felt sorry for her, but the baby was sweet and so tiny. He was a joy.

The Storm

In the fall of 1934 we were three sisters walking to school. Bertha was now the first grader. I was a second grader and Lydia was the big third grader. We always followed Lydia, walking to school single file along the road according to age. I don't know why; we just did it that way.

One night, coming home from school, we saw a big, dark cloud in the sky. It looked fiercer by the minute and was fast coming closer. When we were about half way home we took a short cut. We crawled under the fence and cut across the corner by going through the field. We walked very fast. When Mom saw us coming, she ran out from behind the chicken house and called, "Hurry, you're too slow. Hurry fast!" She sounded worried.

We ran as fast as we could. We just made it home before the storm hit. "Why were you so slow?" Mom said. "When a storm comes up you need to hurry." She was distraught and worried about us getting caught in that terrible storm.

The Axe

Dad told us never to play with the axe that he used for splitting wood. One day when I was seven, I was in the wood house along with my one-year-old brother, John. I saw the chips and the chopping block. I thought how neat it would be to split the chips on the chopping block—just the way I had seen Dad do it. I put the chip on the block, picked up the axe and chopped.

Just then, John reached for the chip and the axe cut a deep gash in one of his fingers. It went clear into the bone. Instantly I realized my disobedience. I took him by the hand, both of us crying and we walked toward the house. I was mortified, as well as horrified that I had cut his finger. I hurt inside for my baby brother. I was also afraid because I had disobeyed. I told my mother John had fallen on the axe. Dad was sent for. When he came rushing home my parents took John to the doctor to have his finger sewn.

When they came back, Dad questioned me, but I stuck to the story that John had fallen on the axe. Dad could not understand how that could happen, since he had left the axe in a position that a child could not cut himself. Dad believed in taking us at our word until proven guilty. He questioned me no more.

I was greatly distressed and miserable, both because I had hurt my brother and because I had disobeyed and then lied about it. Every time I looked at his scarred finger, I felt the pain of guilt. Finally, when I was 11 years old, I could stand it no longer. Now I also felt guilty before God. I told Mom and I wept deep within my spirit, turning my face to the wall. I felt worthless. She said she would talk to Dad about it.

The next day Mom told me Dad said I had suffered enough all these years that punishment from them was not needed. How I loved my Dad for being so understanding. He never approached me about it. The subject was dropped and never again mentioned. He was loving and kind to me, just as usual. I felt completely forgiven and loved. Although I still regretted having done it, the guilt was gone and I felt so free. The big burden had been lifted off of my shoulders. After that I was careful to always tell the truth.

Police Dog

Once Mom sent me to the farm where Dad worked to get butter. We weren't making butter at that time. Perhaps our cow was dry. At the farm they had a "police dog" as we called him. He was a German Shepherd. I was afraid of him as he always barked at us. I was afraid of barking dogs.

When I came up to the house, the dog was lying outside. He did not bark and I felt so good about it that I waved at him! Instantly he jumped at me barking. He jumped up to my head and was about to bite me when I screamed. The dog ran around and around me, barking and jumping as I turned around and around to get him out of my face. The family was in the house eating lunch. When they heard the racket, the father jumped up, ran out and took the dog away from me. I was shaken. I got my butter and went home without seeing the dog again. I didn't go there by myself again.

Moving Day

That fall, Dad rented a farm closer to Dover. We moved the first of January. A day or two before we moved it snowed and was very cold. My parents decided that with all the people coming in and out helping with the move, the house would be too cold for young children. They decided that on moving day Bertha, I, and the two little ones were to go to the neighbors where Dad had been working. Bertha and I were to help watch the little ones and the lady would bring us to our new house after lunch.

I did not like the arrangement. I wanted to see the excitement of moving. Also, Mom had fixed a delicious meal for the folks who helped in the moving. I must have showed my disappointment because the lady tried to cheer me up. She wanted to know why I wanted to go with the movers and I told her that Mom had fixed a good dinner. She told me she would fix us a good meal and I could choose what I wanted. Mom had fixed beans with tomatoes so I chose beans. The lady fixed them with milk instead of tomatoes. I did not realize she wouldn't know how Mom would fix them. I was disappointed but I did not say so.

In the afternoon my disappointment was dispelled. I had a real sleigh ride! When it was time to go home the lady snuggled us together on the one wide seat and wrapped us tightly with blankets. The horse trotted off briskly and the runners glided smoothly over the snow. The crisp air was invigorating. All too soon the ride was over. That was my first and last ride in a real sleigh. I am grateful to that kind lady for such fun!

The New Home

All too soon the sleigh ride was over, but now I had the excitement of walking into our new home. We did not know of the great surprise we would find. We went up the outside stairway, leading into our spacious upstairs apartment. We found a large kitchen, a large living room and four bedrooms. In our exploring, in a back bedroom we found a piano! Someone had left it there. What a great event! Now we could learn to play the piano.

We didn't have lessons but we played around on the piano on our own. We did learn to play a few of the tunes we sang at school. We learned to play them by ear. "Mary Had a Little Lamb," is one of the tunes we learned to play.

When we moved we had to change schools. We went to another one room country school, but we missed Mrs. Massey. Now we walked two miles to school. We finished out my second grade year at this school. At the end of the school year, this school was closed down. We had the summer to play and help Mom and Dad. The landlord, Mr. Derickson, lived on the farm too. He had a fine house out by the road. To get to our home we had to use his lane, going past his house, then the barn. Our house was last. There was also a small apple orchard, but Mr. Derickson did not take care of it. The trees grew apples anyway. The crops weren't large, but the apples were good.

Mr. Derickson also had a long row of black-eyed pea beans close to the orchard. He asked Lydia, Bertha and me to pick those peas. When we brought them to him, he gave us each a quarter. We thought we had a lot of money! Candy bars were five cents each in those days. We could each buy five candy bars. I don't remember what we bought but we thought it was great to be paid for the work we did.

Raising Potatoes

Mr. Derickson did not have cows. We only had one. This was a cash crop farm. Dad was a sharecropper and we raised such things as corn, soybeans and potatoes. I thought we had a huge potato patch.

It was about two acres. Dad hired two or three ladies from the neighborhood to help cut the potatoes for planting. They had to be cut so that each piece had at least two or three eyes to sprout and grow. We watched the ladies cut the potatoes, then watched Dad and a hired man plant them.

There was a planter. Two horses, hitched to the planter, pulled it along the rows. Dad sat on the front seat to drive the horses. The hired man sat on the planter and put a potato down a shoot, one at a time. The planter covered the potatoes. It took Dad and the man all day to plant many rows of potatoes.

The potatoes grew all summer. When we dug them in the fall it was already getting colder. To dig them, Dad used a horse-drawn potato digger. Then it took hired help again to pick up so many potatoes. We girls helped on Saturday when there was no school. By evening it was so cold my hands got real stiff. By then it was soon dark and we were done for the day.

Edwin's Accident

One day some of my brothers and sisters were in the field with my Dad. They decided to come home before Dad did. They came along by the road. There was not much traffic on this road. That day a car did come and the driver tooted his horn. My brother Edwin was frightened and ran out in front of the car. The car hit him. The car headlights broke. The broken glass cut Edwin's head and his leg was broken.

Mom saw Dad carry Edwin in the lane. She ran out to meet them. I ran with her. When Mom saw and heard what happened she cried. I felt like crying too. Edwin's head was bloody and his leg was crooked. Edwin was crying. It had to hurt a lot. The driver drove Edwin and Dad to the doctor. Mom needed to stay with the rest of the children. The lady of the driver stayed with us too. She was saying over and over how sorry she was. She cried a long time. I felt sorry for her too.

Edwin was in the hospital a long time. He had weights to pull on his leg. The weights were on the end of a rope that went up through a pulley above Edwin's bed. The other end of the rope was somehow connected to a contraption on Edwin's foot or leg. This was to pull the bones down so they could move into place. The bone had overlapped the upper bone at the break.

The doctors put Edwin's leg into a cast before he came home. It was like wearing a pair of cast pants. Both legs were in a cast up to his waist so that he could not move his leg at all. It was a bad break.

The cast was on for six weeks and it made Edwin a little fussy. He was only four years old when this happened and he got tired of being in bed. The weather was so warm that with the cast, Edwin was very, very warm. He was fussy and cried at times. We took turns fanning him. We had no air conditioners or fans. We spent a lot of time playing with him.

Finally, the day came when Dad was allowed to take Edwin's cast off. Dad soaked the cast with vinegar water so that he could cut it. He had to cut down the length of the cast. Then the other leg too. I was a little anxious as I watched. It looked dangerous. I was glad when he was done.

Edwin tried to walk, but he couldn't. He had to learn all over again, just like when he was a baby. He didn't have enough strength in his legs to walk because he had not used them for so long. He could only crawl. It was a hard time in Edwin's life.

My Canning Experience

One day I had a bright idea. I had been watching Mom can green beans, beets and more vegetables. I was seven years old and thought I could can too. I found five or six small jars. Then I went to the garden and picked green beans and Swiss Chard. Swiss Chard is a type of greens. I liked them.

I filled my jars with the vegetables and covered them with water like Mom did. I put the tops on and set them along the wall down in the lower part of the house. The jars looked so pretty—just like Mom's. I was so pleased with my accomplishment. A few days later when I checked on them I was disappointed. They were all spoiled, I asked Mom why they spoiled. She said they needed to be boiled a long time and I had not boiled mine. Now I knew it was not something for little girls to do. We were not allowed to work or play with hot water.

This same summer we also heard that Mrs. Massey's brother-in-law died of food poisoning. Mom took us to see Mr. and Mrs. Massey. The brother-in-law lay in his coffin in the best room. He was a handsome man and was engaged to a neighbor girl. I felt sad about his death.

This same summer Lydia and I went to meet Grandpa Bylers at the main highway. They were coming home from market and we had permission to go spend the weekend with them. It was fun to ride in their market wagon. Aunt Lena was only one year older than Lydia and we had a lot of fun playing together.

City School

In the fall we went to the Dover City School. The bus came by our house and picked us up and took us to this huge school. The high school, middle and elementary grades were all on one campus. There were hundreds or thousands of students. Because the country school where I finished second grade had closed down, all the children from my country school had to go to the city school. It was a big, scary adventure to me—a little Amish country girl in this many storied city school. There were so many rooms. There were three rooms just for third graders. I liked my third grade classroom and Mrs. Perry, my teacher. She worked with me to improve my reading and it did improve

In the fall there was a garden show at the school. Anyone who had vegetables to put on display was to bring them to school. We were to bring a vegetable outstanding for its size or another good feature, or anything unusual. I did not bring anything.

Mrs. Perry asked, "Don't you have a garden?"

I said, "Yes, we do"

"Well, don't you have anything to bring?" Mrs. Perry asked.

"We have big potatoes," I said. "But I can't come to the show." The show was the next day, Saturday, and the bus would not pick us up on Saturday.

Mrs. Perry said she would come to my house and get the potato and enter it for me. When she came she said, "Get the biggest potato you can find." I found a great big one.

When I came back to school Mrs. Perry said I had won a prize with the potato. It was a garden trowel. Although at that age I didn't have much use for the trowel, I was pleased to have won a prize. I gave the trowel to Mom so she can use it.

Gideon was born while I was in third grade, on October 12, 1935. Then on October 31st, I turned eight years old.

One morning I got off the bus at school and realized I was lying on the ground. The bus driver and a high school girl were leaning over me, helping me up. I wondered why they were there to help me up. My lips and my cheek were hurting and bleeding a little. They said a boy on a bicycle had run into me from behind me and knocked me down. I must have been knocked out for a little while, as I didn't know anything about it until they were helping me up. The bus driver told the high school girl to take me to the school nurse. The nurse cleaned me up and put ointment and dressings on my wounds.

Mrs. Perry selected about 18 out of the class to start a band. I was one of those selected! We were preparing to play at the Christmas program. We had only simple musical instruments such as flutes and discs. I don't remember the names of all the instruments. One of the boys had two disc-like objects that he beat together in rhythm to the music. At other times he rubbed them together. I had two or three little crimped wheels attached to a stick. I was to shake it at intervals to the music. It had a thin, high pitched, clattering sound. It was fun to be in the band. We started practicing six weeks before Christmas.

Then came a big disappointment. The landlord did not keep his part of the sharecropping bargain so my parents had to find another place for us to live and Dad to work. Before Christmas they found a place and we had to move. When Mrs. Perry learned that we were going to move, someone else had to take my place in the band. I was very disappointed. We girls wished we could wait until after Christmas to move so that we could be in the school program.

Dad said that he would take us to see the Rose Valley School Christmas program. We remembered how much fun the programs were when we went to school there. Lots of people came every year to see the program. We knew our moving couldn't be helped and tried to be satisfied with going back to the Rose Valley program. Still, I was sorry not to be in the band. It was hard to give that up.

Our new home was below Hazelville, about 12 miles south of where we had lived. Dad did not forget to take us to the Rose Valley School Christmas program. I don't remember what was on the program that year, but I remember our long ride to the school. Distances seemed much further because we used a horse and buggy. Dad made it fun for us. It was late when we got home from the program.

After settling into our new home, preparations for Christmas began. We girls were allowed to help Mom make candy. Mom made fondant candy. Some of it she rolled out like you would roll a piecrust. Then she spread peanut butter on it and rolled it up like a jellyroll. Then she sliced the roll in one-fourth inch slices. That was so good.

Some of the fondant Mom flavored with vanilla and some with peppermint. We helped her shape this fondant into little balls. Then Mom cooked chocolate syrup with a little paraffin in it so that the chocolate would harden when it cooled. She gave us each a long darning needle to stick into the balls of candy and dip the candy into the chocolate. We walked two laps around the kitchen with the needle of candy that gave just the right length of time to cool and harden the chocolate. Then we stuck the needle into a window screen covered with wax paper and set over the backs of two chairs. We pulled the needle out from below the screen and the candy was left sitting on top of the wax paper. It took us a long time to do all that. We had lots of chocolate drops as we called them.

Mom also made white and chocolate fudges. Some of the white fudge had coconut in it. Some of the white had nuts. I liked the white fudge the best. We could also help stir the fudge after it was finished boiling and it had cooled to the right temperature. Making candy was exciting, especially since we didn't have candy often, homemade or from the store.

In this, my eighth year, instead of all the families getting together at Grandpa's house for dinner, Uncle Norman and Aunt Esther Swartzentruber came to our house. They had four children. The two boys, Simon and Eli, were a few years older than my sister Lydia. Their daughter Anna was Lydia's age. They were our oldest cousins. Mary was only three years old, five years younger than me. Before Christmas it had rained enough to completely flood the lane in the lower part of our woods. Then it got cold and all this water froze. We spent most of the day skating on this ice. We didn't have skates so we just slid with our shoes. There was little use for skates in Delaware as the ice was seldom deep and hard enough to skate. It was an unforgettable

Christmas day. We always enjoyed the Swartzentruber cousins. They had even brought gifts--a bag of candy for each of us.

Maple Grove School and Life at Home

After New Year's Day, 1936, we started at Maple Grove School. It was hard to be starting in another new school. This was now the fourth school I attended and I was still only in the third grade.

There was no bus for this country school and we walked one and one-half miles along a stretch of road that others also walked. There were some rough boys among these walkers. They enjoyed picking on us. We were not accustomed to such treatment and were afraid of them.

With the meanness of the other walkers and my difficulty with my studies, this was not a good year for me. I made poor grades. My lessons didn't make sense anymore.

I do have two good memories from that school term. I learned about the Wright brothers inventing the airplane. I also learned about Charles Lindbergh's first solo flying trip to New York. It was exciting to know this story is true.

Our teacher taught us a new song. Perhaps I enjoyed it so much because it put into words things that were hard for me to know how to express—the wonder of things I see. Below are some of the lines.

On the Way to School

What a lot of things to see
On the way to school
Squirrels running up a tree
On the way to school.

Squirrels building cunning nests
Robins smoothing down their breasts
What a lot of things to see
On the way to school.

One night when Mom was in the living room taking care of baby Gideon, we girls washed the dishes and cleaned up the kitchen. After the kitchen was in order, we took kitchen utensils to rig up band equipment. When we had attended Dover City School, we had watched the High School Band play and march around the square. We liked what we heard and saw, but it was over too soon. Now we had the idea that we could try our own band.

An upside-down saucepan became a drum. We used a wooden handle to beat on it. Two spoons against each other made a

clacking sound. Large lids rubbed together, then clapped against each otter made another instrument. We also had something to make a rattling sound. The rooms and doorways from room to room were laid out in such a way as to form a circle. We children marched single file from room to room, around the circle, each carrying and playing his instrument. We sang as we went along, clicking, clacking and drumming. We did this to entertain Mom and Dad. They enjoyed it a lot—most likely because they saw our joy and satisfaction in doing it.

Dad had a nasty boil—like an infection on his neck. It was called a carbuncle. It was painful and drained a lot. Finally, the core came out. Later he had a badly infected thumb that needed lancing. They did not have the effective numbing medicines like we do today and it was a viciously painful operation. I hurt for Dad when he told us about it.

When school let out we had a great summer at this new farm. We had lots of fun playing in an old neglected orchard. Three of our brothers were now old enough to run and play with us girls. The orchard was over grown at places. There was also a row of grapes that gave us fine hiding places and plenty of old outbuildings. All this gave us a large play area.

There were beautiful hollyhocks blooming along one side and end of the garden fence. We had a lot of garden that summer and we helped with the garden work. We girls also helped with the housework. We did our work quickly so we could go out to play.

There were a lot of trees around the house. I loved the sound of the wind when it blew through those trees. It made a rushing sound. There seemed to be a lot of breeze at that home and I loved to be out in it and feel it on my face. It felt exhilarating to run in the wind.

While we lived at that house my Dad worked for a farmer whenever he could. The farmer was my Mom's Uncle Will. Dad had a good many miles to get there. He left before we got up in the morning and it was late when he got home. It took him at least one hour on the road. He only earned one dollar a day. In 1936 things were still hard because of the Great Depression.

While living on this farm Dad planted
one or two acres of tomatoes. He bought
hundreds of tomato plants. Dad's brother
Milton, wife Winifred, and their children came
to help plant the tomatoes. Aunt Winifred's
parents, Jake Beacheys, also came to help. In
those days people helped each other with big
jobs. There were not so many modern
conveniences and people needed each other.

Dad took a washtub and mixed soil and
water into sloppy mud. Then he took a handful
of tomato plants and swished the roots in the
mud. This was to give the plants a better start
in the ground.

The men and the two grown Beachey
boys, Dan and Sam, pushed long handled
spades into the soil to make a hole. We called
them the spaders. We older children carried
handfuls of tomato plants and dropped them
one by one into each hole. As we dropped the
plants, the spader pushed dirt around the
plant with his foot. Then we went on to the
next hole about three feet away. Down one row
and up the other, row after row, after row, we
all went until the tomatoes were all planted.

Dad had marked the whole plot off in
squares. The plants were put in the corners of
the squares. That way, when Dad cultivated
the tomatoes he could cultivate lengthwise and

then between the plants crosswise. Dad used a horse hitched to a one-horse cultivator to do this.

After all the tomatoes were planted the men made ice cream. The other families brought the hand-cranked freezers. Mom made the ice-cream mix and had it ready to freeze by the time we finished planting. The ice-cream was so good. Everybody had a jolly good time. The Beachey boys were lively and great talkers. They loved to tease and joke.

That summer we had a large watermelon patch. We used to play around the patch and sit on the melons. There was one extra huge melon that I liked to sit on. It was so round and high! A person can't imagine how huge it was unless they could see it! By that time of course the vines were dead and it didn't matter if we played there,

One Sunday night when our parents invited the families that helped plant the tomatoes over to help us eat that huge watermelon. We three large families ate all we could eat and there was still some left over.

One day Mom made something hot and had set it on the counter. My two-year-old brother Henry, reached up and pulled on the pan handle. It tipped over and poured the hot liquid on his face and head. He had a bad burn and at first, he cried a lot. Mom knew a recipe of flour, lard, and eggs for burns. She made some and put it on the burn. It healed nicely. It seemed to take away the pain. I remember how badly Mom felt that she hadn't set the pan back further and how sorry she felt for Henry and how she ached for him.

New Homes for Some of Us

Times were really getting tough. There was never enough money for what we needed. The church we attended recommended that some of us children should be put out into other homes of the church members for a while so that there wouldn't be so many for my parents to feed.

Albert was to go to Uncle John and Aunt Mary. Later, Edwin went to stay with them instead of Albert. Albert and Edwin were only about four and two years old and it was hard for them to go. One time Uncle John and Aunt Mary brought Edwin home to visit. He cried

when he needed to go back with them. Mom
cried too. But the church said my parents
should let the children go, so they did. Because
the church helped my parents financially
sometimes, my parents felt they needed to
obey.

It was decided that I should go to my
Uncle Amos and Aunt Mollie. I was eight years
old now and could help Aunt Mollie with the
children and do other light household chores
such as washing dishes. On a late August
Sunday Uncle Amos and Aunt Mollie came to
spend the day. When they left, I was to go
home with them. I loved Uncle Amos and
Aunt Mollie and was glad to go with them, but
I couldn't help thinking about the long time
until I would see my family again. We had
moved into another church district so I
wouldn't even see them in church. I went with
mixed feelings.

Their son Crist was a baby, so I helped to
take care of him, playing with him and keeping
him quiet. Living with Amos and Mollie I was
back in our old neighborhood where Dad had
worked on the Hochstetler farm. Uncle Amos
hadn't moved in those years so now I was
back.

One day Mollie sent me to my Grandpa
Bylers on an errand. The horse, Babe, was

hitched to the buggy. Lydia and Florence went along with me and I drove the horse to Grandpa's. She was a safe horse but she could run very fast when she had a mind to. I enjoyed driving Babe. I don't remember what my errand was. I remember the important trust of driving the horse with my little cousins with me. I would still have only been eight years old.

When school started I walked to Mrs. Massey's house to ride with her to school. My cousins were too young for school, so now I had to make this walk alone. It was familiar territory and I didn't mind too much.

I was glad to be back in Rose Valley School and have Mrs. Massey again as my teacher. I was put back from fourth grade into third grade. It made a great difference in my scores. I did well in my grades throughout the rest of my school years. I think starting school at age five was a little earlier than I should have. Some children, like my sister Lydia, could handle that.

On cold mornings our teacher played records. We marched to the music of these records. Marching kept us warm until the room warmed up. One song was about an elephant and butterfly. We bent over clasping our hands, hanging them low and swinging them back and forth, like the elephant's trunk, as we marched.

God's Protection

One day Mrs. Massey arranged to show us a movie about the pioneer days in the house of a neighboring store. The store was in the direction of my home at Amoses. It told of some conflict with the Indians but also of some friendly Indians. There was a beautiful little girl in the movie who seemed to be in the middle of everything. She had a doll that she clung to wherever she went. She lost it or it was taken from her. An Indian found it and brought it to her. Watching a movie was a new experience for me. I loved it but I couldn't understand how those pictures could move and talk!

It was a long movie and was late when we started for home. Mrs. Massey usually picked the neighbor boys and me up on her way to school. "Could you three walk this time?" she asked. "I would like to take these other students home in the other direction." We started walking home. By then darkness was on its way. After we walked a while, it was red in the low Western sky. I knew it would be almost completely dark when I got home.

Just then a car came and stopped. The man asked if we wanted a ride home. The two neighbor boys were ready to ride. They saw I wasn't going to get in. They said, "Come on. We know this man. He is a neighbor."

I didn't know what to do. My parents taught us, "never get in the car if you don't know the people." It was getting so dark and I was afraid of the dark! Oh, what should I do? I decided it would be all right since the boys knew him and he would probably take me home first. Then I wouldn't have to be alone with him.

After more urgings from the boys, I got in on the back seat. The man was talking with the boys as we rode along, and to my dismay, he drove right past my road! After letting the boys out at their house, he drove back to my road. He told me to climb over the back of the front seat and sit in the front with him. "I want to show you some pictures in a book I have," he said. "They are about what boys and girls do." I didn't want to sit in front with him. I didn't want to see his pictures. I didn't know what he was talking about but I obeyed. He showed me the pictures, but they meant nothing to me. I didn't understand them. I was afraid.

When we got to the lane, he turned the car around to head back and then stopped. He begged me to go for a ride the next night. He said he would pick me up when I was walking home from school. I kept saying, "No!" I tried to open the door, but I couldn't get it open. He kept begging and finally after a long time he opened the door for me. Before he opened it, he made me promise not to tell anyone.

I promised and I planned to keep a promise. I had been taught that to break a promise is to lie. I ran home, up the long lane as fast as I could. When I got inside, Aunt Mollie was right at the door to meet me. She asked, "What is wrong?" She could see something had happened. I wouldn't tell. I only said, "I'm not going to school tomorrow."

"I was worried," said Aunt Mollie. "You are so late. Were you in the car I saw at the end of the lane. I saw the lights in the dark."

"Yes," I said. I could not answer her question of who was in the car because I did not know the man. Aunt Mollie did not give up. She kept asking me what was wrong, what had happened. "Your face is as white as a sheet," she said. "Something is wrong."

"I promised not to tell," I said. She assured me that to break such a promise was not to lie. Finally, I told her everything. Again, I said I was not going to school the next day.

Aunt Mollie said, "Yes, you are going to school. I will take you to Mrs. Massey's house and talk with her. I will ask her to bring you all the way home."

Aunt Mollie was upset about what happened. The next morning, she took me to Mrs. Massey's and she agreed to bring me all the way home.

That same morning Uncle Amos went to the store where the movie had been shown to purchase some things. He told what had happened and was told to call the police. He didn't want to, so they said they would.

That day two policemen came to my school. They talked to Mrs. Massey, then with the two boys and then with me. They asked me many questions. I didn't understand why they asked me all those questions and I was afraid and embarrassed. I felt something must be wrong with me. I was embarrassed to be involved and that the other students knew something was going on.

It was all very confusing. I knew something was not right, but I didn't understand it. I only knew it was something I was afraid of. I was too young to fully understand. When I came home that evening Aunt Mollie said the police had been there to talk with them.

Later that evening the police came again and said that they had found the man and locked him in jail. They said they might need me on the witness stand. That really worried me! I did not want to witness. I thought that being on the witness stand meant that I was going to have to sit high up on a stand where everybody could see me. Everything was so confusing. I just wanted to forget about it and not have people talk about it. To my relief I was not called to witness.

The police found out that this man had previously kidnapped two little girls. How glad I was he didn't take me away that night! I am sure now that the Lord was taking care of me the night I was in that man's car. Else, why didn't he kidnap me that night when he already had me in his car? How I thank the Lord for being so gracious to me.

For a long time after that the young girls I played with would ask me about it. I did not want to talk about it and said very little. It all made me feel like I was somehow different from other girls. Finally, I heard no more about it. I guess people forgot it.

A few months later it was Christmas! Aunt Mollie gave me a metal box with a thimble, needles, a pincushion, and eight or so different colored skeins of embroidery floss. I thought it was a most wonderful gift!

Life on the Stoltzfus Farm

I went home to live with my family again after Christmas. It was moving time again because Dad had found better work on a farm. It was New Year's Day when we all moved to a house on the Jonas Stoltzfus farm. Mom fixed sauerkraut, spare ribs, and mashed potatoes that day. It was so good! I don't remember what else she fixed.

Mr. Stoltzfus had two farms: one on each side of the road. He lived on the one farm and we lived on the other. On this farm we could keep our cow, have chickens, ducks, and a pig. We could use the farm buildings that went with the house.

Mr. Stoltzfus had a large house and barn and lots of cows. He kept a mean bull with the cows in the pasture. Mr. Stoltzfus kept a chain in that bull's nose so that when he ran he would step on it and be hindered from charging. He also wore what Mr. Stoltzfus called glasses. It was a ten inch square of tin, which lay over his upper face so he could not see out in front of him. That bull learned to hold his head to one side so that he could see and he would lift this head high so that he wouldn't step on the chain.

I was afraid for the girls that had to bring the cows in. Sometimes the bull would run for them, bellowing. The girls would scream as loud as they could and then he would leave them alone.

Still, I was afraid for them. Mr. Stoltzfus had a water wheel down by the creek. It pumped all the water used on the farm. We

enjoyed going to the creek to watch this water wheel work. My Dad was paid twenty dollars a month. That was a good wage for those days. We had a house rent-free, a big garden and the other benefits I already mentioned.

The Stoltzfuses had a daughter, Emma, who was Lydia's age, and a daughter, Katie, my age. Their next daughter, Rachel, was younger than Bertha. Anna was younger yet, and the youngest child was their only boy, Isaac. There were three daughters older than Emma; Lizzie, Lydia, and Rebecca.

Sometimes on a Sunday afternoon we would get together and play. In the front lawn near our house was a large tree with a  swing. The others spent a lot of time on the swing, but it made me dizzy. I pushed the swing for the others.

We again attended the Rose Valley School. We had about two miles to walk. When it snowed we took milk with sugar and vanilla in a jar for our lunch. At lunchtime we scooped snow into the milk and had snow slush. We liked to call it ice cream.

Sometimes we had cake too, but most often we just had two sandwiches. Often the sandwiches had only mustard, or only margarine and salt and pepper. We didn't have anything else for sandwiches. They were good, toasted at school.

Mrs. Massey allowed the coals in the wood stove to burn down to a red-hot bed. Then the older boys toasted the sandwiches with Mrs. Massey's wire grill rack. This little grill had two racks about 10 x 15 inches that were hinged together at one end. The grill had a long handle. Six sandwiches could be placed on the rack, then the other rack was brought down on top of the sandwiches. When one side was toasted, the whole rack could be flipped over to toast the other side. All who wanted their sandwiches toasted lined up to wait their turn. Usually 30 or so sandwiches were toasted. It made lunch time much more exciting and pleasant.

This was such a happy school. It was like a large family all working and playing together. If there were any arguments or fights Mrs. Massey settled them. She got the offended and the offender together, be it two students or a group of students. She took the time necessary to get to the root of the problem. When she had it settled all knew and recognized it as being settled. There was to be no grumbling or they would all be called back again. Usually they all would be feeling good again. Mrs. Massey had a son in school. She showed him no partiality. I think she could do this because she treated us all as though we were her children.

That winter I went to live with my Uncle John and Aunt Mary Lee. Since Rose Valley School was next to their farm, I could continue to go to school there. I helped Aunt Mary with their one-year-old baby. I also washed dishes, did odd jobs and whatever I could to help.

Farmers' Market

Uncle John and Aunt Mary went to Dover on Saturdays to sell things at Farmers' Market. Thursdays they started baking the things to sell. They baked twelve or more layer cakes and iced them. They also made about four sponge cakes and one or two angel food cakes. Thursdays was also the day to make the apple and cherry pie fillings.

On Fridays, Uncle John made lots of bread and cinnamon buns. Aunt Mary made all the pie crusts, rolled them out, and put them in pans. When school was out for the summer I helped Aunt Mary with the baking. I pressed the flat side of fork prongs around the rims of the crusts. I also pricked the bottoms of the pie crusts that were to be baked before filling. This was to keep the crust from making air bubbles as it baked. After baking the crusts, Aunt Mary filled some with lemon custard and the rest with coconut fillings that the hired girl had made. We made 50 to 60 pies. Uncle John made the white fluffy icing for the cakes. They worked until midnight. I went to bed at my usual time. When I woke up Saturday mornings they had already gone to market.

On Saturdays I helped the hired girl with the cleaning. We had to wash all the baking dishes, pots, and pans from the day before. It took until noon. She washed and I dried. I did not like drying dishes all morning. Of course I also took care of the baby. That gave me some little breaks from drying dishes.

Aunt Mary grew up in the Lancaster, Pennsylvania area. Frequently her relatives came to visit, especially her parents. I liked her parents. They always brought their granddaughter along. The little girl, Annie, was cute and intelligent. Her mother had died so she and her father lived with her grandparents.

Aunt Mary talked a lot about her family and acquaintances in Pennsylvania. I got the feeling that Lancaster people were better people than other people were. I'm sure her new, exciting stories just caused me to assume that.

That fall I became ten years old. Uncle John and Aunt Mary gave me a new, dark red dress. Aunt Mary made it. I was so pleased with it and thought it the prettiest dress I had ever seen.

During these nice fall days, we played in the woods at school. We girls had pretend houses and played family. Our pretend families would visit each other. The boys climbed trees and played games like baseball and work-up. The girls also played kick ball. We had two teams. The base was about 40 feet away from a pole. One team was between the pole and the base line. The other team stood behind the base line and had their turn kicking the ball. We tried to kick the ball in a direction away from the pole so that we had time to run around the pole and back before someone caught the ball and hit us with it. After three "outs" to a side, we changed sides. When the bell rang for classes, whoever had the highest score won the game.

In the fall or spring, we had Field Day. All the area country schools would come together to one school for a day of play. We had organized games and all the teachers had a part. Usually four schools participated. Each school chose a color. Ribbons the color of the schools' choices was tied to the arm of each student from the schools. Now we could tell which school everyone was from. The oldest boys usually had baseball all day. The rest had games suitable for their ages. It was a fun day. I only went when our school was the host.

We had so much fun at Rose Valley School. I enjoyed this school much more than any of the other schools I attended.

Christmas Program

The Christmas programs were always exciting at Rose Valley School. The year I was 10 was especially exciting. We had recitals and songs like usual, but the main program was a play about Mr. Brown's family and their cook. My sister Lydia was the cook and dressed up like Aunt Jemima on the pancake box with a red bandana on her head and a white apron. We made her fat by stuffing pillows under her dress. Her hands and face were made black. Her hair was already black. She played her part well.

The children of the Brown family hung their stockings up and they and all the household went to bed. Shortly after, two boys came downstairs and hid behind a chair to wait for Santa Clause. When he came, one of the boys sneezed. That surprised Santa and he started looking for the boys.

The cook heard the commotion and came upon the scene. It was dark in the house and she couldn't see. She called, "Mr. Brown, Mr. Brown!" She threw her hands up and back, saying, "The burglars are here! Mr. Brown, the burglars are here." Such a frightening ruckus she raised. That alone could have scared any burglar out of the house.

Well, Mr. Brown came running. He switched on the lights and discovered Santa and the boys. Soon the entire household was awakened and they all had a pleasant evening as Santa cheerfully entertained them.

When Santa left the children sang, "Good-Bye, Santa." Santa sang back, "Good-Bye, Children," until his voice faded out in the distance.

Another year, the main program was done behind a curtain. The audience could not see, but could hear the play. The play began with the mother reading an invitation to a Christmas dinner from a well to do family in town. What a great cheer went up from the children. They were poor and had no family near so it was a rare treat to receive an invitation.

Suddenly the cheering stopped as one asked, "What shall we wear?" They realized they had nothing good enough to wear as guests to a richly dressed party.

"What can we do?" wailed Marge.

"My shoes have holes in the soles and are badly scuffed," added Billy.

"Quiet down, children. Let me think," said Mother. "Billy, there isn't anything we can do for another pair of shoes. We will polish the tops and you can keep your feet flat on the floor so no one will notice the holes. Your suit coat sleeves and trouser legs are a little frayed, but they are long enough that I can turn them under and they will look new. I'll bleach the stain out of your white shirt, give you a haircut and you will look like a gentleman."

"Marge, your best dress will look nice if you wear it with my lace collar. I can make a belt of a contrasting color. Tied with a bow in the back, it will be lovely. You have that new pair of socks from your aunt. I'll trim your hair a bit and tie a bow in it to match your belt. You will look your very best."

"As for little Ann, I can take your dress that's too small, the white one with the tiny pink flowers, and make a dress for Ann. With a pink sash and hair ribbon it will be perfect with her light complexion and blonde hair.

With her large hazel eyes, she will be pretty as a picture."

"We'll fix James and Georgie up nice too. I'm sure we'll find something. As for myself, don't worry. I'll have something nice."

"But Mom, all you have is that old brown dress."

"That's okay, Marge. I can crochet a new collar. No, that won't do because the cuffs are sad looking too. I have a bit of turquoise velvet. I'll make cuffs and a collar out of that! That will add color and new life with the chocolate brown of the dress. A black bow of narrow ribbon pinned at my throat will make the dress fine enough. The hat I just did over will be nice with the dress too. I don't have a coat like they wear nowadays but I'll turn the bad side in and the patch won't be noticed. Let's get our things together and start. We have this afternoon and tomorrow to work on them."

The children shouted in delight as they gathered the ribbons, polish and other needed items. They helped their mother all they could, often getting in each other's way so that sometimes Mother had to calm the cries and complaints between them.

By the next evening the clothes were ready. "Now" said Mother, "We must get the wash tubs in, one in the living room for the boys and one in the kitchen for the girls. Billy, you draw the water and pour it into the tubs. Be sure it's warm, but not too hot. You help your little brothers with their baths. I'll do their hair and ears."

We heard the tubs being set on the floor, and water being poured into them. We heard the children calling, "Whose turn?" "Aren't you about done," and "Where are my clothes?"

Hair was braided, little ones dressed, and shoes tied. Everything the family did was talked about and had sound effects so that the audience could follow and know just what was going on. Finally, they were ready, pleased with their dressed up appearance.

"Now children, I want you to be well behaved and polite. It doesn't help to look nice outside if we are not nice on the inside. Pretty is as pretty does. Don't forget."

"We won't, Mom," chorused the children.

Then their ride was outside. They all hurried to the door, shouting, "Here we go!"

"Please children, calm down. Oh dear James, your hair is rumpled. Let me fix it. Ann pull up your socks. Marge, help her. You do look lovely, Marge."

And so they went out the door and that was the end of the play.

After the play, we gave our attention to the Christmas tree. Mrs. Massey's husband had cut the tree and brought it on his truck. There were many shiny, colored bulbs that we had all helped hang onto the tree. There were also candy canes hanging on the tree that would be passed to each of us students after New Year's Day. The final touch on the lovely tree was the shining tinsel.

The older boys passed out the gifts from under the tree. This was a relaxing, cozy togetherness after the excitement and stage frights in front of a whole room full of people. Guests and students mingled and soon it was time to go home. Along with our treasured gift, we were given a bag of candy, nuts and an orange from Mrs. Massey.

"Merry Christmas," Mrs. Massey would say to each of us as we left. "You have all done wonderfully and I am pleased. Thank you! See you after Christmas vacation."

Mrs. Massey was always good at helping us appreciate and enjoy Christmas, and creating programs with good lessons. We enjoyed the many December rehearsals. Everybody did well—except for one dreadful time. I was to sing a solo and have the rest of the students join in for two phrases on each verse. Then we were to sing the chorus together.

There was a long row of Lancaster, Pennsylvania Amish folk standing along one wall. All seating was taken and people just stood where they could, even out in the vestibule and on the porch. Because I had the notion these Lancaster people were better than others, they disturbed me as I stood up to sing. I began with the second verse! And then I didn't know what was next. I didn't realize my mistake for a bit, and I just stood there not knowing what to do. Then I realized what I had done and sang the first verse. I felt like crying and nearly did.

Later I apologized to the teacher. She said she hadn't noticed, but I knew better. She couldn't have missed what I had done. She was kind not to hurt me further by showing disappointment.

While I was living with Uncle John and Aunt Mary I was sometimes able to go home after school with my sisters and brother. A few times I walked home by myself on a Saturday afternoon.

Henry and Pneumonia

It was winter and my three-and-one-half-year-old brother Henry, became deathly sick with pneumonia. He was sick in bed six or more weeks before he could even begin to sit up. The back of his head had something like bedsores from lying down so long. My parents had to shave the hair off the back of his head. He had pretty curly hair, but it had to come off. Few visitors were allowed to see him, not even family! It was doctor's orders.

When Henry couldn't eat he was fed blackberry juice and water with a bottle, like a baby. He could barely even suck. He lay with his hands by or up over his head. It gave Mom hope, because she thought his hands would go down to his sides before he died. Then my parents changed doctors. The new doctor was concerned. One night he feared Henry wouldn't live until morning. He stood by Henry's bed and prayed for him. The next morning when the doctor came out, Henry had made some improvement. He looked at us with big brown eyes and was no longer delirious. He was still too weak to move. Slowly he got better. He was weak and it took a while for him to be able to get up and walk.

I came home one Sunday afternoon with Uncle John and Aunt Mary to see Henry. I had hardly seen him since he was sick, but I was only allowed to be in his room for ten minutes. The door was kept shut and a window was open just a bit to give more oxygen. Although I was scarcely home during that time, I know that it was a trying time for my parents. They were concerned but they trusted God.

They were thankful and grateful to God when Henry got well. Before Henry got well enough to sit, Gideon got sick. The doctor called it TB of the bone. It was a few months before he and Henry could walk again.

My sister, Lena, was born the following January while we still lived on this farm. She was not hearty and strong as a baby. She spit up most of her milk. This went on for three months. She also had diarrhea most of the time. She became sicker and sicker.

One day my Great Aunt Lena said that baby Lena might respond to a formula called Alberta Food. It was put up like dry baby cereal. It was said to be very nutritious. Mom tried it with Lena and soon we saw improvement. Mom put that formula in her milk for a long time. Lena became a normal child, but she was never as strong as the others were. She was always more nervous.

Making Ends Meet

In the summertime Dad had lima beans and a few other vegetables to sell from the garden. Mom also butchered chickens and ducks for Dad to sell in the Fall. Dad had off early on Saturday evenings, around 4 p.m. so he could go to town for groceries. Then he peddled the vegetables and chickens. He went door to door in the residential sections of town and usually sold everything. It was a great help for getting grocery money. His monthly wages didn't reach for our large family and it seemed there were always doctor bills what with Henry and Gideon's illnesses, Dad's surgery and then Mom was in the hospital a few days.

Mom and Dad worked hard. Mom washed with a hand-operated washing machine. It had a foot pedal that pushed a handle back and forth when it was pedaled. This handle turned the agitator back and forth. When we girls were old enough we helped Mom with this work, but we did not enjoy it.

Dad's back had been injured and his foot broken in the early years of my parent's marriage. A car hit him when he was walking home after dark from Grandfather's farm. He had pain the rest of his life but he worked hard anyway.

Keeping our large family in shoes and clothes was not easy. Dad bought leather and repaired our shoes on his shoe lathe. He could do a good job and because of his skill our shoes lasted a long time. When a pair was outgrown, we handed it down to the next child. Mom did a lot of repairs on our clothes. Every week she had a pile of mending to do and did a neat job of it. In the winter there were a lot of stockings and heavy underwear in the pile. Because we walked to school we needed a lot of warm clothes. Our houses were cold too, as they were not insulated in those days. It was warm near the heating stoves but cold everywhere else. As the boys grew, they played a lot on their knees, so the pant knees and seats required a lot of mending. When the patches wore through, Mom took them off and put others on, or sometimes she added patch upon patch. Mom used to joke, "Patch upon patch, with a hole in the middle." All this mending took a lot of time, but there was not money for new clothes. Mom was cheerful about it and even though our clothes were patched Mom kept them neat and clean. Mom canned a lot of vegetables from our garden. She bought and canned fruit. Apples and peaches were ten cents a basket. The baskets were about two-thirds of a bushel.

One weekend when I was home I had a bad toothache. Dad took me to the dentist to have it pulled. While in town we visited Grandma Lee at the Farmers' Market. She gave me a bouquet of flowers she hadn't sold. I asked Dad to sell it for me when we did the peddling. A lady bought it for ten cents and I bought two sauce dishes for Mom with the money.

I was still at Uncle John's when I had my eleventh birthday. They gave me a child's prayer book. I was so pleased with it as I enjoyed books. I had access to very few books other than my schoolbooks so this gift was precious.

Another Move

By New Year's Day my parents needed to move again. The Stoltzfus' oldest daughter had married. She and her husband wanted the house. I came home and moved with my folks. Dad rented a small farm where he could grow a few crops, and keep a cow and chickens. He found a few odd jobs around the neighborhood, but he still needed a main job somewhere. Before we moved into the house, relatives and friends from church helped clean it. I went to help too. I scrubbed a very dirty kitchen cupboard until it was clean inside and out. It took a long time but I was pleased when it was clean enough to put dishes into it.

This new house was large. The wallpaper was coming off in places and there were holes in the walls. Mom cut pieces of old white cloth, dipped it into paste she made from boiling water and flour and put the cloths over the holes, pasting it onto the walls. It dried to a nice white and looked much better. It kept the air out. We didn't have money for real wallpaper.

Wiley's School

From this house we attended Wiley's School. The four-mile walk took us about an hour. That was the farthest we ever had to walk to school. Worse than the walk were the mean dogs and the angry bull we had to put up with along our way. The bull would come to the fence by the road and throw dirt with his feet and bellow. We were always glad when he was in the back of the field. Then he didn't bother us. The bull was about one mile from home.

Just before the school, there was a German Shepherd that was usually tied, but once in a while he was loose and came out to bark at us. I was so scared of that dog! The bull never got out of the fence but I was afraid he would.

Our new teacher was nice and very quiet. She did not mingle with the students much. She tried to see that her students were comfortable and cared about them without saying much. I always had trouble adjusting to new schools. It took me a while to get on with my school work and my grades usually came down. When I adjusted and relaxed the lessons became easier.

For Valentine's Day we had a box decorated with red hearts at school. Everybody put valentines into the box. My parents did not have money to buy Valentines so we made our own. After I ate my lunch, I spent the noon hour making a valentine for each student in the upper grades. I decorated them with hearts and flowers. Every valentine was different. I didn't know if the students would like them, especially since they had seen me make them and already knew what they looked like. I thought it is better than not giving them any. Everyone thought they were nice, after all. That is, the girls did. I can't remember that the boys paid any attention to them. But they got one from me, like it or not.

I remember having the story of Pinocchio in our readers at this school. I liked the story.

In the winter we had to wrap warmly to walk so far to school. We wore boots, rain or shine, to keep warm. When spring came, walking to school was pleasant and fun.

At school the boys played prisoner's base. The girls ran races on the road. Our playground was not large and the dirt road was a better place for running. I usually won the races. We also played tag. The boys played too. No one could catch me, not even the sixth grade boys. I was in the fifth grade then. I couldn't catch them either, no matter how hard I tried. I couldn't run as fast when I was chasing as when I was being chased. I couldn't run fast for long as I tired quickly.

One evening as we walked home from school Uncle John Byler stopped to tell us that they had a new baby girl. We were excited and could hardly wait to get home to tell Mom. I remember having been to their wedding the year before.

Uncle John built a small house on Grandfather Byler's farm. The garden was between them and the farmhouse. This little baby girl was the only child they ever had. She was small and very cute. They named her Sylvia.

Times Still Hard

Times were still hard. My parents did all they could to provide for us. Mom baked rolls and loaves of bread, and cinnamon buns to sell. Dad took them to town and sold them when he peddled. He had some regular customers on his route. Folks also came to our house to buy the baked goods.

Mom washed and ironed clothes for a neighboring family. Every little bit helped to put food on our table, or provide things that were needed.

Lena became quite sick with a cold. Mom rubbed Vicks on her chest and put hot towels over it. On Saturday I sat by the stove with her to help keep her warm and to relieve Mom so she could get some work done. Sisters Lydia and Bertha cleaned the house and Mom had mending to do. Mom made Lena a pair of shoes out of denim and old rubber sheeting. In those days, rubber sheeting was thick and tough and brown. It made pretty good soles. There was no money to buy shoes. I remember that day as being Lena's worst day, but she soon got better.

In late winter and early spring there was a lot of dry land cress in the field next to the house. Mom had us go to the field and pick the cress. She made white sauce gravy with a little vinegar in it. She boiled eggs and sliced them into the gravy, then added the fresh, chopped cress. We ate it hot on boiled potatoes. That was a complete meal for us. Oh, it was so good! It was great to have fresh greens.

Soon school was out for the summer and we could feel free again. I liked school, but summer vacation was better. Then, by the time school started, I was glad to go back again.

One day Mom allowed me to make a doll dress. I think it was a dress for my sister Lena's doll. That was my first attempt at sewing. I had watched Mom cut and sew dresses many times, so I knew a little about it, but she still had to help me some.

Back to Uncle Amos and Aunt Mollie's

After school let out I went to stay at Uncle Amos and Aunt Mollie's again. They still lived where they had. I helped Aunt Mollie with the children, washed dishes, cleaned house, weeded the garden and did anything an 11-year-old could to help. At that time my little cousin Henry was only a few months old.

Sometimes I helped with the cooking. One time when Henry needed her attention, Aunt Mollie had me make brown gravy. She sat by the stove with him and told me just how to do it, step by step. I knew brown gravy had a tendency to get lumpy so I was careful not to put too much or too little milk into the gravy at one time and I stirred real fast. Aunt Mollie complemented the smoothness of the gravy and I felt good at having accomplished it. That was the first difficult food I had cooked, although I could already make easy things like oatmeal.

I liked to spend my free time in the yard. Aunt Mollie had pretty flowers along the garden path. I enjoyed walking there with the flowers. There were lots of trees around the house and yard. Lydia, Florence and I played house among the trees when we had spare time. This was usually an hour after dinner dishes were done. Lydia was six years old and Florence five. They were old enough to be my helpers at playing house. I had no other playmates. They enjoyed playing with me and that was good enough for me.

July 18th my sister Betty was born. She was 11 pounds and a beautiful baby with lots of black hair. I was still living with Aunt Mollie so I did not see her often. That year Mollie canned a lot of peaches and I spent a day helping her and eating a lot of peaches. That night I woke up feeling sick. I needed to get up and go out. We had no modem conveniences. I was afraid to go out into the dark night, but I needed to and quickly! I lost all my supper, but I didn't wake Aunt Mollie. I just went back to bed.

I didn't feel much better the next day and I didn't eat much. When peaches were served,

I did not feel like eating them and passed them on. Uncle Amos noticed and asked if I didn't want peaches, I said, "No, I don't feel like it." He said, "Well, that explains why you are sick!" He may have been right as it was a few years before I could enjoy fresh peaches again.

This was the summer I learned about Japanese Beetles. These beetles like blackberries. When Aunt Mollie picked blackberries we had a hard time keeping the beetles out of the bucket. When the beetles were disturbed, they drop from the bush into the bucket. We had to wash those berries carefully. The berries were black and so were the beetles-almost. They clung to the berries when they were in water.

I didn't like the beetles to cling to my fingers. They gripped tightly and it felt creepy. I don't like insects on me, especially not spiders. I don't like anything that stings.

There were a great many wasps around because of the many trees and old buildings. The wood shed close to the house and the back porch where we washed clothes had so many of them and I was afraid. I threw hot water on the nests on the porch.

Once when I went to the woodshed, one sat on my arm. I was afraid to move. I was afraid it would sting if I did. After a long time, it flew away. Wasps, bees, bumblebees, yellow jackets and hornets were a big problem for me. Oh, and the inch-long yellow jackets. I can't abide them. I run from them all.

Dover School

School started again. Lydia, Florence and I went to Dover School. Florence was in the first grade, Lydia in second and I was in the sixth. That year Dover had a new elementary building. It had a great dining hall at one end of the building. The other end of the dining hall was attached to the old school building and housed the high school. The dining hall served the high school and elementary school.

After lunch the high school students pushed the dining tables and chairs to one end and danced. Sometimes sixth graders were required to sit and watch. They were allowed to dance if they wished, but few of them did.

Mrs. Webb was my teacher. She lived close to Grandfather Byler. Mrs. Webb was a good teacher. She expected much from her students, not only in their lessons but also in their behavior and manners. She was a no nonsense teacher but was quick to praise a student when deserved.

There had been some trouble with boys picking on girls out on the playground. The teacher made a rule that any "mismove" a boy made toward a girl was to be reported.

One day after recess, when we were lined up to file back into the building, a boy in the next line snapped his fingers toward me. I thought nothing of it. He was a nice boy and I didn't assume that his finger snapping was intended to annoy me.

Another girl saw what happened and told the teacher. I did not think of it as anything to tell. The teacher told me to come out in the hall with her. Then she went to the boy's room and brought him over and asked me if he was the boy. I had to admit that he was. I was embarrassed. The teacher asked me more questions, but I don't remember what they were. I told her what he had done was really nothing. I was afraid he thought I had done the tattling. He was required to apologize before he went back to his room.

On the school grounds was a large building called the Field House. It was about 300 feet from the school building and was used for special functions such as plays and recitals. The high school students were putting on a play. The parents were invited. Elementary school children and their families were also invited. Lydia, Florence and I did not have money for tickets to attend this performance.

When school was out I went to meet the bus like usual, but Lydia and Florence didn't come. I knew that their teacher had bought tickets for them so that they could see the play. I thought surely the play should have been finished by the time the buses came! As I waited, I worried more and more about the girls. I knew I couldn't leave without them. I decided to go find them.

I walked across to the Field House but wasn't sure which door to go in. There was a big door at the side and a smaller one at the end. I finally chose the smaller one. It opened into a narrow hallway, which lead to another room. The door to that room was closed. On each side of the hallway there were doors that were open. I didn't know what to do! About that time a girl dressed as a pioneer came into the hall from the right. At the same time an Indian came from the door to the left.

I was stunned and frightened. I didn't know what to do. He had feathers on his head and paint on his face. The Indian just stood looking at me, as if he wanted to know what I was doing in that hallway. He then crossed the hall and entered the door to the right. I learned later that the door to the left was a stage entrance and the one to the right was the dressing room.

I realized I had come into the building the wrong way. I wanted to get out of that hallway and quick, before anyone else saw me standing there. I was still quite shaken from the appearance of that Indian.

I went to the door at the end of the hall. When I opened it I found everyone seated in the auditorium. I panicked and just stood still. Mrs. Webb was sitting close by. When she saw me, she came to see what I needed. I told her I needed Lydia and Florence, that the bus had come. She told me the bus would wait and that I should sit with her. She bought a ticket for me at the ticket table and we sat down. My worries were over. Everything was taken care of. The girls were safe and the Indian was gone. I was grateful for my dear teacher.

As I look back, I think I only missed about half of the play and I enjoyed the part that I saw. I could enjoy it because I was a safe distance from the Indian, and because I now understood he was an actor, not a threat.

Uncle Amos had a driving horse named Babe. She had a trick of breaking away from the horse stall if she was given the chance. One time she ran out and Aunt Molly tried to head her off. The little children were playing outside the barn at the time. Babe ran right over one of them, but the child was not injured. Aunt Mollie was shaken up. She thought sure the horse had killed her child.

One Sunday morning I had permission to go home for the day. My walk would take me through the pasture, the woods, and across the fields of a farm on the other side of the woods. Then I would be only a few miles from home! Just as soon as the breakfast dishes were done, I started off with great anticipation. I enjoyed going across the meadow, along the creek, and among the scattered trees. It was a lovely, peaceful morning. I followed the path through the woods and soon came to the fence near the edge of the woods that separated the two farms. I had to crawl under the fence to follow the path.

Once on the other side of the fence, I noticed a herd of young heifers watching me. I suppose I startled them for suddenly they broke into a run and headed right for me. I ran back to the fence and crawled under as fast as I could. I didn't know what to do next, as I so much wanted to go home. I hadn't seen my family in quite a while. I didn't want to give up but I knew I couldn't get past those cows. They stayed put on the other side of the fence, just staring at me. There wasn't anything to do but turn back. It was a lonely walk back to Uncle Amos and Aunt Mollie. When I went into the home I explained what had happened. I felt like a fraidy cat. Uncle Amos told me that the curious heifers wouldn't have hurt me. Then he kind-heartedly walked me back and helped me get past them. I finished my journey alone, arriving home about noon. It was so nice to be home.

On that visit home my sister Lydia told me that food had been really scarce. She said sometimes she and Mom went without breakfast. Mom felt that Dad needed breakfast more than she did since he had to go to work. Dad had to leave for work before the rest of the family ate breakfast so he didn't realize Mom was going without. Lydia also gave hers up, because the school children needed their breakfast. Lydia didn't go to school right away that fall.

I felt sad that they didn't have enough food. Times were so hard, but what could be done about it? At that time things could be purchased from Sears on credit, so our winter clothes were bought through the Sears Catalog, on credit.

On this same visit Mom told me that Lydia had been suffering with abdominal cramps. Even though Mom did all she knew to do, nothing seemed to relieve the pain. The attacks would come and then go and come again in a week or so. These hard times concerned me. I felt guilty that I was not at home to help bear the burden. At Amoses I had plenty of food and I was healthy. I wished I could share my food and health.

Mom and Dad took me back that night with the horse and dearborn. They had no buggy at that time. I was glad I didn't need to walk back. That meant I was able to stay longer.

Around that time Jake Miller's wife Sarah died. She left behind six children. The oldest ones were the ages of we older ones. In the past, we had had so much fun playing outside with those children. Now they had no mother. Her funeral was on a Sunday. Uncle Amos and Aunt Mollie attended the funeral and I stayed home to care for my cousins.

I had a happy surprise when my parents came home with Uncle Amoses for the noon meal. They talked about Sarah's sickness. Her cousin Nancy had taken care of Sarah and the family. Nancy stayed on to help after Sarah died.

About a year later Jake married Nancy.
It was a good arrangement. The children
already knew her. She was a good mother and
wife. Some years after Jake and Nancy
married, we lived at Brenford and were
neighbors to them. By the road it was three
miles or more. It was much shorter to walk
across the fields. We walked the railroad track
to cross the river that separated our fields.

At school Mrs. Webb had my reading
class teach the lower level reading class 15
minutes after school. About three weeks before
Christmas she said she would take all the
helpers to Wilmington to do Christmas
shopping. At Easter she would take the lower
level class. I thought that was nice of her.

Mrs. Webb lived near my Grandfather
Byler's. I spent Friday night with
Grandfathers. The next morning, I met Mrs.
Webb by the road. I had only ten cents to
spend. It seemed the other students had a lot
of money and bought a lot of things, mostly
trinkets. I bought a pretty pink glass relish dish
for Mom's Christmas gift.

The day seemed long as we went from
store to store, everyone trying to decide what
to buy. There were many more stores in
Wilmington than there were in Dover and it
took a long time. We had a lot of fun. I was

glad Mrs. Webb took our reading group first because after Christmas Uncle Amos' moved to Grandfather Byler's farm and I would have missed out on the shopping spree.

Grandfather Byler's Farm

It was nice being close to Grandfathers on their farm. Uncle John and Aunt Mattie had built their little house at the other end of the garden by the road. Then they moved away. Grandfathers moved into the little house that Uncle John built and Uncle Amoses moved into the farmhouse. Aunt Lena was two years older than I was. Aunt Lydia and Aunt Eva were also still living at home with Grandfathers but they were some years older and soon married. Because the little house was so small, the three girls came from grandfather's house each night and slept in a bedroom that was kept for them in the farmhouse.

The receptions for both weddings were in the farmhouse. It was a lot of work to get the house and food ready. Grandma always made large sugar cookies for receptions. I loved these cookies. She sprinkled sugar on top and stuck a raisin into the middle of each cookie. They were soft with a crispy top. There were many good things to eat, but I remember her sugar cookies the best. She also made these cookies for many other occasions.

That winter I developed a painful ear infection. Uncle Amos took me home to stay until it healed. There was another time I needed to go home for a week. Aunt Lena and I had decided to plant a flower garden out by the road. We prepared the soil, digging and raking, all the while anticipating the beautiful garden full of flowers. At some point, I stepped on the rake that was lying on the ground, prongs up.

The prongs went deep into my foot. The wound became infected. I had to stay off my feet and was taken home to recover. We did not have many flowers planted. After my accident we just sort of gave up on the garden. After that I was more careful to keep the prongs of the rake downward when laying or setting it aside.

Living at Grandfather's we attended Miss Webb's sister's school. We cut across the field to walk to school. This Miss Webb was different from the Miss Webb in the Dover School. She didn't involve herself in student conflicts. She expected the students to solve their own problems. She also didn't push us to get good grades. I still tried just as hard because I wanted good grades.

The playground was smaller than any school that I had attended. It was not large enough for a decent ball game. There were trees in the yard, making even less room for a game. Sometimes the boys went across the road and played ball in the field. Sometimes we just played catch. We had more snow than usual that winter and had many good snowball fights on that little playground.

My cousins, Anna and Mary Swartzentruber came to this school. To me, the rest of the students were strangers. We students were allowed to go to the blackboard to study our Math and Spelling lessons. Sometimes several of us would be at the board at the same time and we would help one another. Some days we went to the board that was hidden behind the stove. I thought it was more fun there, being hidden.

One day Miss Webb brought a bundle of skeins of what appeared to be flax yarn. The skeins were all a natural color. She had us take some of it home to dye. I dyed mine purple. She showed us how to weave handbags with the yarn. We all brought our home-dyed skeins and put them on a table. Then we could each choose as many colors as we wanted from the pile. We used both the natural color and our dyed colors for our designs. I enjoyed that project. The girls got along better when we worked on projects than when we had playtime.

Miss Webb had the older school girls take turns to stay after school and clean the schoolroom. Two of us worked together each evening sweeping the floors and cleaning blackboards. She paid us each five cents a night. Sometimes a girl wouldn't be able to take her turn and I was happy to take it for her. Then I was able to do the cleaning two or maybe three times in one week. I was so glad to earn the extra money. Later in the year my mother needed to get fabric to make new church dresses for Lydia, Bertha and me. I was glad to loan her the money I had to help buy the dress material. The fabric cost about 25 cents a yard. Our everyday fabrics were not nearly as expensive at about 10 cents a yard.

Mary Jane was born on July 9th. With a new baby there was much more work. Aunt Mollie and Uncle Amos hired a 16-year-old girl to help with the work. She and I made a good team. I liked her. Her name was Mary Jane too. She later married my cousin, Simon Swartzentruber.

In the summer I sometimes worked outside for Uncle Amos. Lydia, Florence and I would work together herding cows for a few hours each day. After the hay was made, the cows were turned into the hayfield to graze. There were not fences around the hayfields. That's why we needed to herd the cows. That was a job I really enjoyed.

Sometimes I harrowed with a spring-toothed harrow when Uncle Amos was getting ready to plant corn. I liked harrowing. First Uncle Amos plowed, then disked the field. Then three horses were hitched to the double-set harrow. I followed behind the harrows, driving the horses. First I went over the field lengthwise, then diagonally, then crosswise. It took a lot of walking to follow that harrow. I was tired when it was finished, but I liked to be with the horses out in that quiet field. I liked seeing the field now ready to be planted and knowing that the horses and I had put the finishing touches on it.

I also helped Uncle Amos in the hayfield. After the hay was cut and partially dry, he raked it into rows. Then he used a three-prong pitchfork and made the rows into small piles. I had another fork and also made piles. When we were done making piles Uncle Amos hitched two horses to the wagon and they walked along the rows of piled hay. As Uncle Amos forked the hay onto the wagon, I tramped it down tight. Sometimes I needed to fork the hay evenly in place on the wagon. By tramping it down we were able to get much more hay on the wagon. Sometimes Lydia and Florence helped with the tramping.

When the wagonload was so high that Uncle Amos couldn't reach the top of the hay, he got on board and drove to the barn. We helpers rode on the very top of that huge pile of hay. What fun it was to be up so high and see all around.

The upper floor of the barn was for storing the hay and was called the hayloft. Uncle Amos had a good way of getting the hay way up there. In the hay loft there was a hay track high in the peak of the roof. Attached to the track was a big forklift to pick up huge bunches of hay. A door in the end of the barn loft was opened for the forklift to come out and down on the load of hay. The wagon was placed in position for the fork. A rope was attached to the forklift, along the track

following the peak to the other end of the
hayloft, and out the upper door. The rope was
brought down to the ground and fastened to
the double tree. The double tree was fastened
to two single trees. These single trees and the
double tree were not trees that grow in the
yard, but implements used to hitch horses up
to farm equipment.

When we brought the wagon of hay into
the barnyard, the two horses were unhitched
from the wagon and each hitched to one of the
single trees. Now they could pull the rope
fastened to the double tree. When the fork
came over the hay wagon, Uncle Amos
fastened it to a big bunch of hay. I took up the
horses' lines and drove them forward to pull
the rope that would bring the forklift full of hay
clear across the track to the other end of the
barn. When it got to that end the fork tripped
and let go of the hay. By then the horses and I
would be at the far end of the rope. Then I
turned the horses and went back to the
starting point and headed them in the
direction to go again. As I came back Uncle
Amos pulled the fork end of the rope onto the
hay again. As I was driving the horses back, I
had to be careful not to allow the rope to slack
or it could bump against the horses' feet. This
could hurt and scare them. I could not really

enjoy this part of hay making because the danger of allowing the rope to slack worried me so. To prevent the slack, I sometimes had to lift the double tree. It was heavy. I wished I didn't have to drive the horses for this part of the haymaking.

This procedure had to be repeated again and again until the wagon was unloaded. Then we went into the hayloft and tramped down the hay. After that we hitched the horses to the wagon again and went to the field for another load of hay. I enjoyed working in the fields. It could be hot and tiresome, but it was good exercise and invigorating. I sometimes became very tired, but I liked the outdoors.

I also tried my hand at milking but I never accomplished much. I never milked more than one cow and that took me a long time. My hands always got so tired. Lydia and Florence, especially Florence, had better rhythm with their hands than I did. I milked the Guernsey cow. She was the one I liked best. She was gentle and had a pleasing personality. All the cows had their own characteristics and personalities. One small Jersey cow was quick witted and had a will of her own and a mean streak to match. That meant we had to be quick too. I liked her in spite of her faults. I thought she really did look intelligent. When she wasn't performing one of her mean capers, she was good.

I was in the seventh grade then. The country schools only had grades one to six. I would have had to go to the city school or to one of our church schools. Our church schools had grades one through eight. At that time, we didn't have to have more than an eight grade education. I went to our church school.

It was too far to walk so I went with my Swartzentruber cousins, Eli and Anna, in their horse and buggy. Another cousin of mine lived just up the road from us. We met Eli and Anna out on the main road to catch our ride. That buggy ride meant we had to walk less than a mile.

I started to school late in the year so that I could help Amos with the fall work and to baby-sit when Aunt Mollie went with Uncle Amos to the field to husk corn. When she went, I stayed in the house and took care of the little ones and cooked dinner.

I started school in October. In December we had our Christmas program. On the blackboard I drew the picture of the wise men coming to see Jesus. They were riding on their camels with the star above the stable to guide them. Shepherds with their sheep were nearby in the field. I used colored chalk for the drawing. I always liked the Christmas programs. The parents came to school for the programs.

When we went to Rose Valley school we had more opportunities for programs and for acting. Mrs. Massey made fun for us and let us act out the stories in our readers, such as, "The Three Bears". I was Goldilocks because I had red hair.

One time we played Hansel and Gretel. For the witch's house Mrs. Massey had the boys go to the woods close to the school for tree branches. She stuck marshmallows, lifesavers, cookies and gumdrops on the tips of the branches and twigs. Hansel and Gretel were to eat of these treats. After we finished with the play, Mrs. Massey divided all the candy among us children. All of the students played this one. Those who had no other part pretended to be the fence around the house. At the end the "fence" came back to life and helped eat the candy.

Uncle Amos' Move to a New Farm

Uncle Amos found a farm that was bigger than Grandfather's farm. It was 10 miles to the northwest of us. We moved there in January. Kenton was now our closest town. I could not go to school there with Lydia and

Florence because the school only went to sixth grade. They rode the bus. I would have needed to ride another bus and go to the Smyrna School, which was eight miles away. I could have gone to the North Church School. That would have been four miles and I would have had to walk alone. I did not want either choice, so I asked to not go at all. My wish was granted. This meant that my formal education ended after three months in the seventh grade. When I was in my forties I studied and passed the test to earn my GED.

In the spring of 1941, the United States joined the allies in World War II. Without radio and newspapers, we didn't hear much about the war. Sugar and gas were rationed and we had to have stamps to purchase them. Draft age men and boys had to register for the draft. Farm buildings were allowed to be built but no new houses.

About the time Amoses moved to the Kenton area, my parents moved west of Kenton. Going by the road and through Kenton we had about four miles to my parents. If we went across our fields and a neighbor's field, we had only one or two miles. This made it easier to visit my family. I could walk.

My parents' house had only two rooms downstairs and three small rooms upstairs.

The landlord promised to close most of the porch that ran full length along the back of the house. This was our new kitchen. He also promised to build a dairy barn against the other barn. He did both of these when the weather turned warmer in March 1941.

My brother Simon was born that winter. He had a digestive problem until he was at least a year old. Mom put bismal powder in his milk to help him. One or two weeks before he was born I went home to help with the work. I was now 13 years old. The night Simon was to be born, Dad took me to Uncle Amos' after he called the doctor. He took Aunt Mollie along back to help with the birthing. Simon was born before the doctor arrived. In those days doctors did deliver babies at home. When Aunt Mollie came home the next day, I went home again for a few weeks to help my sisters with the work.

I needed to patch stockings. This was my first time patching stockings and Mom didn't allow me to do it without a thimble. She said I would never learn to sew with a thimble if I didn't use one in the beginning, no matter how cumbersome it was for me at first. I sat close by her bed and she coached me.

Back at Uncle Amos', the house was fairly big, but old and cold. We had lots of trees. There was a horse barn, a dairy barn and a granary. Uncle Amos converted the upstairs of the granary into a chicken house.

In the mornings Aunt Mollie helped with the milking. I got breakfast and looked after the children as they woke up. I also packed school lunches for Lydia and Florence.

Aunt Mollie taught me to sew, starting on easy things like hemming tea towels, making pillowcases and a few simple garments. I liked to sew more than most other tasks and chores.

One night Lydia and I went to stay with an older lady who lived half a mile down the road. Her husband had died and she wanted us to keep her company until her children came the next day. It was a cold night. She gave us a feather bed to sleep in. I got very warm that night. I was far too warm and couldn't sleep well. The next morning when I awoke, I was sick. I thought I got a fever from being too warm in that feather bed. Maybe I was too warm in the bed because of the fever. I did manage to walk the half-mile home. I spent the day in bed. The next day I felt better but still wasn't over it. Amos' were butchering then and I couldn't help.

The beef was killed the one day and the carcass hung on the back porch to freeze overnight. The freezing was a way to tenderize the meat. It was great to have the delicious fresh meat. We had no freezers so we had fresh meat only when we butchered. We canned our meat to keep.

When we butchered pork we had cured hams. That was as good as fresh meat. Sometimes we fried sausage in casings and the spareribs. We packed these in crocks. Then we filled the crocks with hot melted lard. The lard sealed off any air space and kept the meat from spoiling. We had to eat that pork before warm weather, as it would keep only while it was cool.

Washing at Uncle Amoses

Washing on cold days was a cold job. We had a gasoline engine washing machine. We had to keep it on the porch so the exhaust stayed outside. Some people had a washhouse and had a hole in the wall. They stuck the exhaust through to the outside. They also had their big iron kettle in the washhouse to heat the water for washing. The kettle was large enough to hold enough water to fill the washing machine and have enough left for rinsing the clothes. More water could be added later to wash the colored clothes. Heating the water also warmed the washhouse. The kettle was fitted into the top of an iron metal jacket and a fire was built underneath it. A stovepipe went from the jacket to the chimney, just like for any stove. It had a door to feed the wood into the fire. The whole thing stood on a cement platform. That was how some folks had it when they washed.

We didn't have a washhouse and the kettle for heating water was outdoors. The water needed to be carried out to the kettle and back to the porch again to the washing machine. Our pump was also on the porch.

I got very cold washing on the porch, but worse yet was to hang the clothes outside. My hands became so stiff I could hardly pin the clothes on the line. My fingers did not want to function when they were so cold. Often small articles like socks were hung inside the house. On very, very cold days we didn't wash. We waited for a warmer day. In Delaware we didn't have long spells of that terribly cold weather. It was broken up with some warmer days in between.

Often in the winter four-year-old Crist got ear infections. He would get very sick. In those days people didn't go to the doctor for everything like they do now. The doctors didn't have the antibiotics to help with infections that are available now. Penicillin was not available until sometime during WWII. Aunt Mollie took care of the infection herself. There were home remedies that we don't know about now. Now doctors take care of things like ear infections with antibiotics, which are usually faster cures.

Crist sang a lot. He started when he was 18 months old. He also liked to take any toy apart to see how it was made and how it functioned. Of course he could not put it back together again! He liked to tease his sisters.

Henry was quieter. He was my little boy, since he was the baby when I came. For a year after I left, when I came to visit he always wanted me to hold him.

Mary Jane was seven or eight months old by now and I thought she was the prettiest baby around. I liked to show her off after church. I was too shy to boast about her, but quietly mingled with people, feeling good about her beauty.

Barbara Ann was both good natured and quick tempered. She was either one or the other, nothing in between.

Florence was the boss of her own life and she let the others know it, myself included. She was also a lot of fun. It was only when she had one of her stubborn spells that she was hard to deal with.

Lydia was usually agreeable and pleasant, but nervous and easily distressed and anxious.

How did I fit into this family? I tried to fit into everything and everybody. It wasn't always easy, but I survived and adopted them all as family. I think, having been living among people, I sort of did according to wherever I was and whomever I associated with. I learned to adapt to others and the situation I was in.

Gardening and Preserving Food

Spring came with its warm weather for our spring work. The fields and garden were plowed. Aunt Mollie and I planted the garden. One day Aunt Mollie went away with the horse and buggy and said I should hoe the garden while she was gone. I didn't need to hoe the whole garden, but some rows near the fence and the flowers.

My mother came for an unexpected visit while Aunt Mollie was gone. She came out to where I was working and saw that I was doing a sloppy job. She took the hoe and showed me how I should draw the soil around the plants and smooth the soil and not leave pockets or holes in the soil were the air gets in and dries the soil around the roots. I knew that, but I was in a hurry to get done. I usually did my jobs well, but that day I wanted to hurry and get done more than I wanted to do a good job. After that, though, I was sure to have my jobs well done.

Later in the summer, when the watermelons were ripe, Uncle Amos would come in from the field at 4 p.m. to do the chores. He would go out to the watermelon patch and select a good ripe one. He would bring it under a tree where we would all gather to eat the melon. They were delicious! It was a pleasure being together in the cool shade of the trees eating that melon. Together we could eat a whole watermelon if it wasn't too big. Sometimes we could eat two, eating only the good middle since there were plenty of melons in the patch.

Rhubarb grew out by the garden. When blackberry time came around, Aunt Mollie went to pick blackberries in the mornings. In the afternoons, she canned what we didn't eat. She also cooked blackberries with rhubarb and thickened it with tapioca. That was so good! Rhubarb is tart and blackberries are less sour, making them a good compliment to each other. Aunt Mollie also made blackberry dumplings, blackberry pie, and rhubarb pie. What good deserts she made with the fruits.

Sometimes I went along to pick blackberries. The nicest, biggest berries were right in the middle of the tangled vines. We had to tramp a path into that prickly patch. Once a path was made it was easier the next time we came to pick. We got many scratches on our arms and legs. We got chiggers too! The chiggers itched badly and were worse than the scratches. In spite of it all, I loved to be out in the woods picking berries. There is something about being in the woods that gives me a feeling of peace and stability among the big, strong trees. There are nice surprises growing low on the ground—interesting little plants and at times unusual mushrooms. In Delaware we did not need to be concerned about poisonous snakes nor dangerous animals. There were none.

Crist had a problem with getting his pants wet because he didn't take time from play soon enough to take care of his needs. One day Aunt Mollie told him she is going to put a diaper and a dress on him for punishment. Boys used to wear dresses before they were potty trained. Aunt Mollie put the dress on Crist and he cried. After a while it was too much for me. I got his own clothes and put them on him. I told him boys don't wear dresses. He still remembers that and talks about it sometimes when he sees me. He was so glad I put his own clothes on him.

One day when Aunt Mollie was away all day, she had asked me to sort through three baskets of peaches and can all those that were ripe enough. She didn't think there would be many. There were enough to can 21 quarts of peaches. I canned them all, in addition to taking care of the little ones and getting lunch. I started around 9 or 10 o'clock and the last cooker of peaches was on to cook by 3 p.m. Aunt Mollie must have thought that was pretty good and told my mother. When I went home for a visit, my sister, Lydia, said she thought she could do better than that. She tried and did, canning more quarts in less time. Lydia always had been a fast worker.

Happenings that Summer at My Parent's Home

My parents had turkeys that summer. When I'd come home through the fields, I needed to come through the barn lot to get to the house. One of the turkey gobbler's pride got ruffled up when he met us. I was always afraid of meeting him. My sister, Lydia, had no fear of him. The gobbler was particularly mad at her because she would stand outside the turkey house window and tease him, stamping her feet and waving her arms. She would insult him, saying, "Gobble, gobble, gobble." When he was out, he would go for her. She would not run, but wait until he got to her, then grab him by the neck and throw him aside. He'd come again, but he could not win and would finally give up. Lydia enjoyed teasing him. I could never tease like that. I was too fearful and it was kind of mean.

Mom had a beautiful little flower garden close to the house. Dad built a fence around it to keep the chickens out. Dad loved flowers too. Mom had beautiful gladiolas. Salmon colored ones were her favorite. She had what was called Chinese Lanterns. These fascinated me. It was the first time I had ever seen any. They were like little orange balloons and did resemble Chinese lanterns.

I loved watching the flowers and the vegetable garden develop. I still love to watch growing things today.

When the carpenters were building the dairy barn where my parents lived, my four-year-old brother Gideon climbed up those rafters that formed the roof then onto the peak itself. The carpenters weren't there and Dad wasn't around at the time. Mom was frantic. She knew she must not show her fear. She calmly called to him to come down. He skipped along the barn roof like there was no danger. What he did when he came to the rafters I don't remember, but he did get down by himself. He loved tools from the time he was a baby. Dad said maybe he would grow up to be a carpenter—and he did. He has always been a carpenter.

My parents had neighbors down the road a bit. Mr. Jim Pinter and my dad shared work at times. They became friends. Uncle Amos and the Pinters also became friends and sometimes all three men shared farm work.

That fall, in October, Allen was born to Uncle Amos and Aunt Mollie. Because sister Lydia was older than I, she came to help Aunt Mollie and care for the baby. I went home during the two weeks Lydia was with Aunt Mollie.

During those two weeks I helped Dad with corn harvesting. Mr. Pinter came and drove the corn binder that cut the corn, grabbed the stalks and tied them into bundles. I rode on the back of the binder and dumped the bundles. Dad followed and set the bundles into shocks. Binding the corn was a new experience that I enjoyed.

When the corn was shocked, I helped Dad shuck the corn. Dad took the bundles from the shocks and laid them on the ground in a circle. We started at one point, each taking a bundle and shucking the corn out of the husk in which it grew. We had a shucking tool strapped to our gloved hands. We ripped the husk back, grabbed the ear of corn, and broke it off the stalk. We threw the ears of corn onto a pile in the center where the shock had stood. Dad was a cheerful person to work with.

On Saturdays my sister, Bertha, and two oldest brothers helped. Dad said he could shuck corn faster than we all could pick up the ears. We didn't think he could, but I knew there was a trick somehow. We agreed to try. So he shucked and we all started gathering up the ears of corn. True to his word, we were not fast enough, for he threw the corn in all directions. We soon gave up and Dad had his laugh. We did not mind his tricks. They were all in good-natured fun.

We all had fun out there in the cornfield. Sometimes we would find nests with baby mice. Although we didn't like mice, those tiny pink babies were so cute and I didn't like having them killed.

When I went back to Aunt Mollie and Uncle Amos I helped him shuck his corn. When Aunt Mollie was stronger, she helped. Then I stayed in the house to look after the baby and the other little ones and get dinner.

Shucking corn was more fun, I thought, so long as it didn't get too cold. I couldn't tolerate a lot of cold weather. I still can't. I turned fourteen that fall.

Near Christmas Aunt Mollie wanted to go Christmas shopping. Allen was only a few months old so she had to take him along to feed him. She took me along to care for Allen while she was shopping. I stayed at the Farmer's Market where both my grandparents and other folks I knew were. Uncle John and Aunt Mary were still selling at Farmer's Market so they were there. Sam Hertzlers were always at Farmer's Market. Every time I was there he would give me a rind piece of cheese with a large section of cheese on it. He brought a whole wheel of Swiss cheese to sell. It was warm at the Farmer's Market and a good place to keep baby Allen. It was around 11 a.m. when we got to Farmer's Market.

Aunt Mollie sometimes stopped in to see if the baby and I were getting along all right. We started home at three. It took us more than one hour on the road to and from town. On the way home it suddenly started getting colder. Aunt Mollie was concerned about her baby getting cold. She hurried the horse. The last two miles the baby cried all the time. I could have cried along with him and I suppose Aunt

Mollie felt like crying too. She looked grim and anxious.

I covered him completely under the lap blankets. Still he cried. When we got home we hurried to the house with him. We could see he was cold but not as cold as Aunt Mollie feared. If she had expected the weather to turn colder, she would not have gone to town.

After Christmas, my parents moved to Brenford, a tiny village with only four or five houses left. The store was closed and the train station was no longer in operation. The farm my parents rented was better and larger than their previous one. The railroad track ran through the farm about 600 feet from the house. There was also a river that ran along our farm. This farm was about five miles from Uncle Amos and Aunt Mollie.

New Jobs/Homes for Me

When spring came in 1942, Aunt Mollie thought she should do without me so that her girls would learn household duties instead of depending on me. I went home, then soon went to help at my mother's cousin's home, the Alvin Yoders. This place was only a few miles from my parents and the same river ran through Alvin's farm that ran through my parents' farm.

One Monday morning I was walking to Alvin's after spending the weekend at home. I saw their three horses come running toward the river. They were hitched to the hay wagon. I was almost on the bridge when they reached the river next to the bridge. I held my breath. I could see they are run away horses. Are they going to stop in time? There was a high bank there. They stopped, just in time! Oh, no! They lost their balance and fell sideways into the water. They were still hitched to the wagon.

The horses looked so frightened and it was horrifying to watch them fall in. There was nothing I could do to help. Alvin came running. Noah Yoder from across the road came too. They jumped into the river and unhitched the horses from the wagon. Then they were able to get the horses out, safe and sound. It is dangerous to get horses untangled when they are scared and wild like that, but neither the horses nor the men were hurt.

After working for Alvin Yoders two or three months I went to work for my Uncle Clarence and Aunt Sylvia Mast. Aunt Sylvia's heart was not strong and she had many headaches. Their children were Lawrence, Daniel (Danny), Lillie, Irene, John and William (Willie). Willie wasn't two years old yet. He was always hanging on to his mom and did not want me at all. After I wasn't such a stranger to him, he didn't have to hang onto his mother. Later Clarence and Bobby were born. Four of these children entered the medical professions; Willie and Clarence became doctors. Lillie and Irene became nurses.

That summer, my parents had a field that had not been tilled for a long time. A portion of the field was covered with dewberries. Mom canned 100 quarts of those berries. Aunt Mollie and others in the neighborhood also came to pick and can berries.

One Friday afternoon Aunt Sylvia sent me home to pick and can for her. Saturday I picked. Lydia and Bertha helped and Mom canned as we picked. We had about 30 quarts. Monday I went back to Aunt Sylvia's with the berries. I had enjoyed the weekend at home.

Aunt Sylvia couldn't help much with the work but I enjoyed the stories she told as I worked. Aunt Sylvia did most of the cooking.

An old man worked for Uncle Clarence. This man remembered his father having been a slave. He remembered seeing long scars on his Dad's back from being whipped. Uncle Clarence had a large tomato patch and hired pickers. We supplied their noon meal. There were usually three to six pickers.

One day that summer on a Sunday afternoon I was at home alone and tried to ride Lawrence's bicycle. I had never tried one before. I was doing pretty well until I fell over with the bike onto some barbed wire. I only had a few scratches but thought, I really shouldn't try riding when I'm alone. If I should get hurt, there would be no one to help me. I put the bike away. To this day I never learned to ride a bike.

One afternoon Aunt Sylvia had a light heart attack. She had numerous attacks through the years. She called me to her bedroom and had me loosen her clothes. She was cold. I heated towels and put them on her feet. When the towels cooled I had another set of hot ones ready to put on. I did not know what to expect. I was worried about her and glad when Uncle Clarence came home and took over.

Willie wanted his mom but I could not allow him in to his mother. He cried. I didn't know what I should do with him because he never wanted me. I picked him up and carried him to the rocking chair and rocked him. He stopped crying and soon he was asleep. I was surprised that he made no fuss about it.

I needed to get supper. I was so nervous that I could hardly accomplish it. I don't know what I fixed. I could hardly think what to cook. It took me so long because my brain just didn't want to function with all the stress. The next day I was sick and had those pains in my side again. I think it was because I was worried about Aunt Sylvia. The doctor came to the house to see her. Sometime the second day I felt better and could come help with the work. Uncle Clarence had stayed around to take care of the family when I couldn't. Aunt Sylvia was soon a lot better.

I was home for a week or so and saw how thoroughly Mom enjoyed her chickens. Mom had an incubator that held 100 eggs. She had to turn the eggs every day and sprinkle them with water. She also had three or four hens setting in the barn. Some hens already had chicks. These chicks and their mothers, called clucks, were kept in coops with pens for protection. Mom soon had about 200 chicks.

The watering trays needed to be washed every morning. Every few days the coops and pens needed to be moved to a clean spot. Chickens may get sick if you don't keep everything clean. There were about four coops with a cluck and her dozen or so chicks. I loved to be out there with her and watch the chicks. I wanted to help her. She said I could give the clucks water that were in a coop by themselves outside the chicken house. These clucks wanted to lay eggs and set on their nest so they could have chicks too, but Mom did not want them to set on eggs yet. She kept them separate.

I did not go water them right away. Then I went in to wash dishes and forgot the clucks. After dark, Mom asked if I gave the clucks water. "No," I said. I felt ashamed of myself. I had forgotten to do it. "I still will." I felt sorry for those chickens. It was a warm day and I was sure their water had not lasted all day. I took the lantern, went out, and gave them water. I sat with them for a while with the light so they could see to drink, but they didn't. I was afraid of the dark, but I was more concerned for the clucks. At least, now they would have water to drink when they woke up in the morning.

One Sunday cousin Lawrence and I walked across the fields and through the woods to Grandfather Byler's house. There was a stream we needed to cross. We went up the stream until we could jump it. Lawrence jumped first so he can catch my hand if I can't make it. Then I was afraid to try. He said, "You can do it," and urged me to jump. I did!

Lawrence was two years younger than me, but he was companionable and we had a pleasant trek.

One Sunday Aunt Sylvia invited my parents for dinner. They brought a few of my younger brothers and sisters along. The day seemed too short. It had been a long time since I had seen them. I was away from home so much of the time that I felt more like a visitor than a part of the family. I sort of forgot my family's way of doing.

My brothers and sisters were growing up in my absence. I did not know them well anymore and did not know much that went on at home. They told me some of the things that happened, but that is not the same as seeing the day-to-day happenings. It made me feel lonely even when I was at home. Possibly they also felt like they did not know me anymore. I often felt so different from them. I developed a personality and characteristics all my own by staying with so many different people.

I had my fifteenth birthday on October 31, 1942. It was around the time of my birthday that Dad and Mom attended church one Sunday where I regularly attended with Uncle Clarence and Aunt Sylvia while living with them. After church, Mom asked me if I had a black dress. I said, "I do". I guess she couldn't remember since she didn't see me often and wanted to be sure I had one.

3 LIFE WITHOUT MOM

On November 16, 1942, two weeks after my birthday, Mom and Dad went to get more sugar stamps. Because of WWII sugar was rationed and you had to have stamps to get sugar. We were only allowed a certain number of stamps per person. If you canned fruit you could get stamps for that also. Many people used Saccharine or Karo syrup for sweetening because there wasn't enough sugar.

When Mom and Dad got the stamps in Cheswald, there wasn't any sugar left in the town. They went to Kenton to see if sugar was available there. By then it was dusk and the road was busy. A car came from behind and drove right into them. Dad and Mom both flew off the dearborn. Mom landed on the edge of the pavement, on her head. Dad raised his head and looked over to where she laid. He crawled over to her, felt her pulse and called her name. She took a few deep breaths and was gone.

The horse stood beside Mom, his broken leg dangling. Dad urged the horse to move over a little. When the police came, they shot the horse. Dad and Mom were both taken to the hospital. Dad was hospitalized with his back hurt again and one of his kidneys torn. Someone from the church was notified and a few families went to my home to tell them and to stay with my brothers and sisters.

Around 10 p.m. a car horn blowing awakened me. Then someone knocked on a downstairs window. I heard voices. Then the car left. Uncle Clarence called me to come downstairs. When I came he and Aunt Sylvia were in the living room. No one said anything. Finally, Uncle Clarence said Dad and Mom had a wreck and Dad was hurt pretty badly and that they didn't know if he would make it. He did not say that Mom was killed. He probably didn't have the courage to say it, nor did Aunt Sylvia. She looked so sad and was crying. Clarence called his hired man to take me home and also to see if Uncle Amos and Aunt Mollie knew about it. Uncle Clarence went with the hired man and me.

When we got to Amos' house, someone was already there. Aunt Mollie looked so grieved that I guessed one of them was killed. Aunt Mollie went with us to my home. On the way, Aunt Mollie told me Mom was killed. I already was too numb to have much feeling. I did not cry. She tried to comfort me.

When we got to my home, my brothers and sisters were all in bed. By now it was past midnight. People were standing around in the house. I just stood there not saying or doing anything. Finally, someone said I could go upstairs to the others. They were in bed.

When I came up my older sisters were not asleep. We talked a little while before I went to bed. How sad we felt but there wasn't much to be said. I did mention my regret at all the years I had to be away from home and not be with Mom much. Only now did we realize how much we loved her and how much she meant to us.

Simon, the baby would not be two years old until Feb. Sister Lydia was 16 and I came next. There were eleven of us. The next day a lot of people came. Most of both our parents' brothers and sisters were there. Other people came to help with the work. The men did the barn chores. The women cooked the meals and whatever else needed done. The grieving family was not expected to help much.

Those days until the funeral were long. I had not brought my clothes along from Uncle Clarence's house so Aunt Mary had someone take us to get my clothes. Then we went to see Dad at the hospital. He was so sad. He was getting better. The doctor said Dad could not come home for the funeral. Dad begged to go home the afternoon before the funeral. The funeral was the fourth day after the accident because of the many that would come from a distance.

I was in the kitchen when they brought Dad into the living room. I was feeling too distraught with grief for Dad to go in to meet him. I thought, I can't face it. Soon someone came and told me to come in. I went but nothing seemed real. The house was constantly full of people and I was so weary. I wished we could be by ourselves for a while. I was tired of acting brave when I felt crushed. I needed to be alone so that I could work through my feelings.

After Dad was home, a small lady came to the front door and knocked. Lydia opened the door. The lady asked if Dad was home. Lydia said, "Yes," and invited her in to Dad, who was lying on the cot. The lady kneeled down by the cot saying, "I am the wife of the man that killed your wife." Then burying her

face in her hands, she wept. Dad wept with
her. All who were in the room wept. After the
weeping subsided, she said, "I'm so sorry, so
very, very sorry."

Dad said, "Nothing can bring my wife
back, but I don't want you feeling badly about
it. It is not your fault. You cannot help it and
are not to be blamed." She soon left and we
never saw her again. Not long afterward,
someone bailed her husband out of jail.

Mom was brought home before Dad. She
was put in the bedroom, still on the stretcher
the undertaker brought her on. One of the
ladies made her a white dress to wear in the
coffin. Mom was washed and ready to be
dressed when they brought her home. They
had washed her hair as well. Her head had
been quite bloody. She had bled from her ears
because her head was crushed inside. There
were no bruises or cuts outside. Her hair hung
loose down over the head of the stretcher. Her
hair and face were so lovely, even then. I
thought she looked as beautiful as an angel.
She did not look dead. She looked ready to
smile. Because her face was not bruised she
looked natural.

Sister Lydia and I were looking at her by
ourselves for a while the afternoon they
brought her. It was comforting to look at her,

but still she was not alive and that was a reality we had to face. We could never speak with her again and soon she would be laid away and gone, never to see her again. The truth, we realized, was that she was already gone. Gone from her body and we knew she was with Jesus. It gave me a peaceful feeling to know she had gone to heaven, a place that is more peaceful and desirable than this world, free from the cares of this earth. She was in a place where all is love.

But, the fact remained, we missed her. We still wanted her. We needed her. We wanted to be with her because we loved her. Now we couldn't. That was final. So final. We could go to her someday, but that was not now. We needed her then. The reality though, was death. I resigned myself to accept the fact the best that I could. Dad was not able to go to the funeral, but he was home in time to see her before the funeral. Aunt Mary stayed with Dad. She told me later that she treasured the quiet time to talk with him. Dad was not able yet to be up and around. His bed was set up in the living room. I know it was a trial for him not to be able to go to the funeral but he did not complain. He has never been a complaining man.

One of the men from church took us to the funeral in our dearborn. It was a cold, drizzly day. Because John Beachy and his wife Emma had a very big house, the funeral was there. Around four hundred people came to the funeral. The viewing took a long time. After the funeral, at the graveyard, my great-aunt Lena requested that we children be allowed to see Mom again before she was buried. The casket was opened again and we saw her for the last time.

The family, relatives, and out of state people were invited to a meal prepared and served at John Hochstetler's home. They also had a big house. After the meal, we were taken back home. It was a long day and I was cold from traveling so much in the cold, damp weather. There were still people at home to get the evening meal. All the next week people came and helped us with cooking, but most of all to sew for the boys and do whatever was needed. They bought fabric for shirts and denim for pants. Food was still being brought in. We were alone on the weekend. The following week they came again and finished up the sewing. There were usually four to six ladies that came. Dad was up and about now, helping with the chores.

Saturday I started getting pains in my side. I could not finish cleaning the kitchen floor. Most of the day I had this aching pain and sometimes sharp pains. I could hardly stand up straight. To clean the floor made it worse. We had no floor covering and had to scrub the wood floor with a broom and soapy water. We followed up with clear water and mopped the floor dry. It was hard work. Sister Lydia finished for me. Sunday in church it still hurt. We were invited to dinner at the house where the church service was held. I was having a difficult time with pain but didn't tell anyone. I don't know why I didn't tell. The only time I said anything was when I was scrubbing the floor. Monday was better.

Tuesday a few women came again to sew. All day my pain was worse. In the afternoon I also started getting sick but still I said nothing. It took effort not to appear sick and in pain. That night Aunt Mary spent the night with us. She slept with sister Lydia in one bed and Bertha and I slept in another bed in the same room. In the night I had chills and was so sick to my stomach I had to get up and lose yesterday's food.

Aunt Mary woke up and realized I was having problems. She got up to do what she could for me. The next morning, she took me to the doctor. He gave me medicine and told me to go to bed. Now I occupied the bed in the living room. A few days later I was worse. Dad called the doctor out. The doctor thought it might be my appendix and took me to the hospital himself.

The surgeon wasn't sure and kept me in the hospital a few days. He decided it wasn't appendicitis and sent me home with medication. I think it was my nerves since after that I would get sick like that when under extreme stress.

We were now on our own. I think that is why I could get better. I could relax more without all the people constantly around us.

There was talk among the people about taking the younger children into their homes. Dad and we three older girls said, "No indeed." Never is this thing going to happen. We girls were taught how to cook and clean house and had always helped with the little ones. We could do it. There were three of us, so why not? And we did. Maybe we weren't as efficient as Mom but we got along.

Dad was always cheerful. I know it was for our sakes. He missed Mom very much. He did not talk to us about it. When he was away on business he would go to Uncle Amos and Aunt Mollie to talk with them after their children went to bed. We did not know he went there to grieve. Aunt Molly told us later. She said he just needed someone to talk with and to tell how lonesome he was. He told them he often couldn't sleep until nearly time to get up. Then he would go to sleep and oversleep. I wish he had talked with us about it. I think we all would have felt better. Just as he didn't talk to us about his aching heart, so we older girls didn't talk much about Mom to the little ones, thinking that would help them not to get so homesick. I know now that was the wrong way to handle it. They cannot really remember Mom. Some of them can remember an incident or two. Perhaps talking about her would have kept her alive in their minds.

One day soon after Mom died, the neighbor girl, Betty Clampet, said the train engineer came to see them. He was a friend of theirs. The engineer asked what happened that Mom wasn't waving anymore. When they told her, he was sad about her death. He said he missed her. Her waving had broken the monotony of the day for him and he always looked for her. They had never met and did not know each other. Neither dad nor we children had ever met him either. We children did see him up close a few times when we were down by the railroad. We kept waving to him.

I still went to the doctor once a month and got medicine. One time I had to wait my turn so long it was almost dark when I started home. Worse yet, my lantern was empty. I had to walk nearly half a mile to the highway to get kerosene at a service station to fill the lantern. I could not go on the road without a light. When I finally got back to the buggy and on the road it was late. Before I was out of town my light went out. I lit it again but soon it went out. I kept lighting it again and again. Finally, I gave up. The wind just blew out the flame. Whenever a car came I pulled off the road the best I could and stopped until the car passed. I was worried and afraid alone in the dark without a light.

When I was within a mile of home I met Dad walking toward me. He said he was worried about me and came to find me. I was so glad to see him. I was not afraid anymore. The lantern remained a troublesome lantern. We used a flashlight and he said he needed to put another lantern on the buggy.

Dad bought us a pressure cooker for canning so that the vegetables could keep better. We planted a lot of vegetables that spring so we had more than usual for canning. We canned lots of peas, corn, beans, and other fruits and vegetables. The peas did well. It was a lot of work to pick all those peas and shell them. We ate all the peas we wanted fresh from the garden. They were so good. The rest we canned.

One morning a fish peddler came to our house. Dad bought some for dinner. This was my first experience cleaning fish. They were delicious. In Delaware the fishermen came with the fish early, around 9 a.m. The peddlers start peddling their fish right after they are caught. They keep the fish on ice all the time and have them sold by noon. They are sold fresh and are much better than fish out of the store.

When baking, my sister Lydia usually baked the cakes and I baked the pies. I liked better to bake pies and was glad she preferred to bake cakes.

Dad needed a pair of dress pants. I made them out of wool fabric. Because wool scratches and perhaps to keep the fabric cleaner, they needed to be lined. It took a lot of concentration to cut and sew everything to come out to fit nice. I guess I did okay. Dad did not complain about anything.

Mom had always cut Dad's hair. It soon became my job. I enjoyed cutting hair. Sometimes I cut little Simon's hair, but usually Dad did, as well as all the boys' hair. There were a quite a few new experiences for us girls in keeping the family going.

In the last years Mom lived, she had a gasoline engine operated washing machine. Now it was worn out and we washed with a washboard. That meant putting the washboard into a tub of hot, soapy water and scrubbing the clothes on this ribbed board. Later Dad had a surprise for us. He did not have the money to buy one like we had before with the gas engine, but he bought a nice little washer that we hand cranked. It was lightweight metal and easy to handle. We liked our little washer and were thankful not to have to scrub by hand anymore. When Dad saw how happy we were with it, he was happy too. Our pump to get water for washing was outside, close to the washhouse door.

One day when we girls were out working by the washhouse, a man came to see Dad. We told him Dad was not at home. He said that he wanted a drink. I went into the house to get him a glass of water and brought it to him. He asked Bertha to show him the pigs in the barn, saying he wanted to see about pigs to buy. Bertha said no. He became disgraceful in his conduct. We went in the house and closed the door. He hung around outside for a little while, then left. We were shocked at such behavior and glad none of us were alone.

The landlord furnished us paint and wallpaper to paint the whole house and paper the upstairs walls. The floors were painted too. Dad put floor covering on the kitchen floor. We painted our iron beds white. Dad bought a little white dresser for our room and we papered the walls a light blue. Mom had bought us blue and white striped bedspreads. When we finished fixing our room we felt we had a lovely room.

One day when I went shopping I saw a boy with red hair. He had blue eyes. How pretty, I thought. If I could have blue eyes to go with my red hair, I might like my red hair. But, I didn't have blue eyes and my red hair kept being a problem to me. Looking back, I know it was the happy glow on his face, much more than the color of his hair and eyes that put beauty on his face.

My freckles bothered me even more than my hair. I had seldom seen anyone with red hair and nobody had so many freckles. I felt uncomfortably different. Later, when I was older I decided not to worry about my looks. I enjoyed happy, friendly, delightful people more than perfect features. I am sure others do too.

Sam Hertzlers made a thick book of, "Words of Cheer," Sunday School papers and gave it to us to read. I read all of it and enjoyed it so much. There were many good lessons in the stories. It helped me get a better perspective of life and the importance of a clean moral life and Christian behavior.

Dad got a few jobs here and there when he had time off the farm. Wages were better now, 80 cents an hour. We thought that was pretty big money. It was far more than the dollar a day he used to earn.

Bertha and I went to town to do some shopping. Our last errand was at the drug store. As we went in we noticed a soldier standing along the show window. When we came out, he was still there and followed us as we started down the street.

We were headed for our buggy, three blocks away in a residential area. He kept asking us questions. He said he wanted to ride with us. We were scared. He may have been perfectly harmless, but many soldiers at that time were not considered safe and the youth and children were not allowed on the streets after dark. That was a city law because of the soldiers.

After following us two blocks he left. We started off in the buggy and then stopped at an

intersection where there was a service station.
This same soldier was there and saw us. He
walked out to the buggy as though he were
going to get in and said he wanted a ride.

The street was clear of traffic now. I
quickly turned the corner and down the street
leaving him behind. Later, when I told Aunt
Sylvia about this she said that I should have
used the buggy whip on him. I asked, "You
mean hit him?" She said, "Yes, for something
like that, it is all right to hit him."

One day Lydia and I went somewhere
with the horse and buggy. As we went along
one of the lines broke and the front end of the
line was dangling down toward the ground out
of my reach. The other end, the left line, was
still in my hands. I could not drive with just
one line. The horse kept going to the left. There
was a deep ditch on the left side of the road. I
was afraid the horse would take us so far
across the road that the wheel would go in that
ditch. I kept hollering, "Whoa," and tried not
to pull on the left line at all. Finally, he got so
close that I got frantic and grabbed the horse's
tail. I pulled and said, "Whoa!" Then he
stopped. A man was in his garden hoeing. He
came out and repaired the line for us. How
glad I was that he was there and helped us.

Fall came and I turned 16. Uncle
Clarence and Aunt Sylvia sent me a Bible with
my name in gold on the cover. I was so pleased
and read it a lot.

Cool weather came. Dad bought us a
new cook stove. How we rejoiced over that
new stove. For years the old one was
troublesome. It was so old; we had to keep
patching up the cracks and holes so the fire
could burn properly. The new one worked
much better and was so pretty.

It was corn-harvesting time again. This
year Dad had more corn and entered a corn-
shucking ring. Neighbors gathered together to
do each other's corn. After the farmers had
their corn cut and in shocks, the neighbors
banded together with a corn shucker. They
moved from farm to farm. Men went to the
field and gathered the shocks of corn onto the
wagons. They were brought to the barn where
the corn shucker stood. They fed the bundles
of corn stalks into a trough-like hopper with a
conveyer to move it into the chopper. The
chopper took off the ears and chopped the
stalks. The corn was separated from the stalks
into a shoot that threw the corn into the
corncrib. The chopped stalks were thrown out,
forming a pile to be used for feed or bedding.
An engine was used to operate the shucker by

running a belt from the engine to the shucker pulley. It saved a lot of time compared to shucking all the corn by hand like we did before.

All of the youth from our area churches joined together for hymn sings on Sunday evenings. We got to know every one of the youth. One of these boys got caught in the belt of the shucker when they were shucking their corn. It killed him almost instantly. That was a shocking tragedy. We all went to the funeral. It was so sad.

In the spring my Uncle Harvey died and a month or two later, my great Aunt Annie died. She died in her sleep. All these deaths in a row, so close together were almost too much for me to cope with but I kept my feelings to myself. The following summer, Emmanuel Spicher from church, was killed when hauling grain to the elevator.

Mrs. DeShong, a neighbor back where we used to live, became almost blind and was not feeling well. She needed someone to stay with her. I was with her for about six weeks. Because she couldn't see well, her house needed a lot of cleaning. Every time we had chicken for supper, Mr. DeShong pretended he couldn't find the heart. He said that I had swallowed it raw so that a boy would ask me for a date.

We had many hard thunderstorms in the night while I was there. The storms made me nervous. One weekend their daughter and her husband came to visit. They saw the house clean now and they liked my cooking. They wanted to take me to the city with them when I finished there with their parents. He said they would give me a good time in the city. He told me there were a lot of nice and interesting things to do in the city. It sounded so good I almost wished I could go. I knew though, that I didn't really want to. I would be in a strange place, not knowing anyone and I did not want to do all of those things he said we would do. I wasn't used to that kind of life. Of course I didn't go.

Lydia, Bertha and I went with Lydia's friend to the river. We could not swim. I disappeared in the water and my sisters could not see me. Then I surfaced. I could not stay up or get myself out. I was helpless in the water and may have drowned if Bertha had not come to my rescue. After that I stayed in the water's edge. I still do not want to go more than knee deep into water.

The summer I was 17 years old, we children all got the measles. We had the

thrashers for the barley and wheat thrashing.
They needed to be cooked for and we were all
sick except Lydia and me. Before dinner we
were getting sick too. Lydia was getting sick
before I was. It was hard to cook for the
thrashers being sick and weak.

After dinner we had a lot of dishes to
wash because we had cooked for at least 10
men and the family. Lydia went to bed before I
did as I wasn't as sick yet. I finished the dishes
and tried to clean the house a bit. I also needed
to look after the sick ones. Some were already
feeling better. Later in the afternoon I could no
longer stay up. Dad came in after the thrashers
left and saw our situation. He hitched the
horse to the buggy and went to get one of his
sisters. Aunt Lizzie came.

Bertha was getting better now. Lydia and
I kept getting sicker. Lydia had a fever of 104
degrees and mine was a little higher than that.
Lydia said I was delirious and talking about
things being on the porch roof outside our
window.

Dad called the doctor. He said to feed us
ice cream and give us ice water and to put a
comforter on us. It was hot summer! The
comforter brought the measles out and we
were soon getting better. When Lydia and I
were well enough to be out of bed, we soon

washed our hair. When we combed it, we combed out a lot of hair. We had a great pile of it on the floor where they landed when we combed. We had lots of long hair so we still had enough left. We were told we lost the hair because of the high fever and that we got so sick because we didn't go to bed soon enough.

The mumps followed soon after the measles. I was in the instruction classes at church for baptism. Dad did not want me to get sick and have to miss classes so he took me to Grandfather Bylers when we discovered we were starting with mumps at home. I did still get them, but I was not as sick as the ones at home. They were all down with the mumps so Dad went for help again. This time Aunt Ivy came. Grandma Lee sent along some medicine called Green August Flower. It was so bitter that they had a problem keeping it down when they took it. They started with very small doses, slowly increasing the doses. Soon they started getting better. Bertha and Lydia got the mumps last and were very sick. Edwin was seriously sick.

When I was well enough I went home to take over and Aunt Ivy went to her home. Lydia, Bertha and half the children were still in bed but they were all getting better. I was glad for that. There was still a lot of work caring for everyone and I needed to get right to work, but soon everyone was well again.

Later this same summer I went to the Lancaster, Pennsylvania area to help out at Uncle Elam and Aunt Florence Fisher. I also worked some for Uncle Rueben and Aunt Lena King. The two families lived about ten miles apart. I worked a few weeks for each of them. Uncle Elam and Aunt Florence had four boys and no girls. Uncle Elam had a blacksmith shop a short distance from the house. When it was warm I took peppermint tea to the shop for him. He said the peppermint cools him in warm weather. The boys were at interesting ages, from one to five years old. I enjoyed them.

Uncle Rueben and Aunt Lena did not yet have any children. It was a lot of fun working with Aunt Lena as she wasn't much older than I was. Their washhouse was attached to the house. They had spring water piped into the washhouse. There was a large trough made of cement and closed in like a cabinet with doors. The spring water flowed constantly through the trough. The water was always cold and fresh. It made a cool place to keep milk, butter, eggs and other foods. Everything was put into tight containers to set into the water. There were also shelves to set containers of food. The doors were kept closed to keep the cool temperature inside. It was almost as cold as a refrigerator.

Back home I also worked for Uncle Andy and Aunt Eva. They had a new baby girl and I took care of her until Aunt Eva was stronger. It was a great pleasure bathing such a tiny, perfectly made body. She was so fragile and sweet, so perfectly dependent on someone to do everything for her. They named her Evalena and her daddy would often sing, "Sweet Evalena" to her. They had two other children, Menno and Mollie. Over the years they had three more children.

Someone gave us two or three of the Elsie Dinsmore books to read. I loved those books and Elsie. She had such high ideals and always came out victorious at the end of her problems and heartaches. She remained firm in what she understood to be right. She frequently suffered for her beliefs but she remained faithful. That is what I admired about her. I also admired her prayer life, perhaps more than anything else about her.

Henry, Gideon and Simon needed new suits for church. I took it upon myself to make them. Now I wonder that I even dared to try, but it needed done, so I did it. I went to Grandmother Byler to get some pointers on cutting and sewing them. Henry's suit was gray and Gideon's was brown. Simon's was black. I thought they looked so nice in their suits. Perhaps the feeling of satisfaction in accomplishing the difficult task added to my impression of their looking nice.

My instruction classes for baptism were over in August. There were about six others in the class with me and were baptized along with me. It was a special day. I thought I never felt so free and happy before.

Lydia went to town with Dad one Saturday and came home with pretty, light, dusty blue fabric for a dress. When Dad saw how Bertha and I admired it and wished for one too, he hitchhiked back to town and got more fabric so we could each have a dress like it. I hope I sufficiently thanked him for doing that. I really did appreciate it. It was too far to have the horse go again, but he was able to catch a ride to town and back again. We three girls often dressed alike.

Dad was happy when he could make his children happy. That is the way he was with Mom. He had a sacrificial love and kindness and I know I did not appreciate him as much as I should have. When you are young you don't think about that as much as when you are older. I often wish I could talk with Mom and Dad about things I ignored back then. I know God will give them their reward and I am thankful to God for rewarding them.

In the fall I worked for Aunt Sylvia some months again. Her fourth son, Clarence Jr., was born during this time. At Christmas they invited Dad and the rest of our family for Christmas dinner. We all enjoyed the day, even though Aunt Sylvia missed Mom. It was sad for her, yet she was pleasant and joyful.

Lydia worked two weeks for Bill and Marion Wetter when they had their third little boy. They also already had one girl. Soon after they moved three miles away onto a farm. Sometimes they came and picked us girls up to come visit them, then brought us back home. We always enjoyed the Wetter family.

My brother Albert worked for a farmer whose land was across from us. Albert worked for the farmer over a year, but always came home at night. He would have funny stories to tell. Albert was a fun-loving person in a quiet sort of way. He was considerate of us girls and helpful. Edwin too was a willing helper.

One night when we girls went to the farm where Albert worked to pick tomatoes for pay, we thought we heard a bull. We stopped and listened. Yes, it was a bull bellowing and coming closer through the cornfield. We took off running as fast as we could up the field lane to the buildings. By the time we got there, Albert called us from the other end, from where we had just run. He came running up to us laughing and said, "Oh, I didn't think you could run so fast!" He said we ran faster than he thought possible. He said, "There wasn't any bull, it was me". He just wanted to scare us a little. He didn't think we'd be that scared. He certainly had sounded like a bull and we weren't taking any chances. We had to laugh with him.

Dad built two chicken houses, twenty feet by twenty feet. Each house held 500 chicks. We fed them four months then sold them at broiler size. After cleaning the houses, we put baby chicks in again. In April Dad thought we could make more profit if we butchered the chickens and sold them in town. So each Friday we butchered fifty, starting when they were fryer size. Saturday he took them to Farmers' Market. If they didn't all sell by late afternoon, he went door to door and sold the rest. When the chicks were four months old we had to sell the rest alive before they got too big.

We had a lot of fun as we butchered the chickens. Dad, we three older girls, and the older boys all butchered. The younger boys,

John, Henry and Gideon could help pluck the feathers. There were enough of us to keep things lively. We did get tired of it but it still needed to be done. Lydia went along to the market to help sell. I went in her place once, but I did not really like the selling part.

One time Albert and I went to town to do the family shopping. We stopped at a store and were trying to decide on a butcher knife. A clerk came along to sell us one. He must have thought we were newlyweds as he said something about needing such things when starting housekeeping. We did not tell him differently and we did not buy the butcher knife. After leaving the store we talked about the fact that it probably is a bit unusual for a sister and brother to be out shopping for household items. It struck us funny to be thought of as married.

Dad came home from town one day and said Aunt Saloma is sick in bed and they need someone to help out. Dad promised him one of us would come. Uncle Elmer and Aunt Saloma's son Noah would come and get one of us. It was decided that I should go. I did not want to go but I did not say so. I didn't know how I could do everything with Aunt Saloma in bed and the children all quite small yet. There were at least eight children and there would be all the baking and other things that needed to be done for the market besides the regular housework and cooking. I didn't know at all how they did things at their house.

On the way to their house, Noah, though quite young, tried to keep a friendly conversation going. I could barely keep the tears back, so how could I talk. I needed to keep my face turned away from him at times. I felt mean about not being more sociable. After a while I felt better and hope I was more sociable. At least he did not appear offended. He seemed happy that I was coming. When I got there everyone gave me a warm welcome. The oldest daughter, Mary, was delighted that she could help me by telling me where to find whatever I needed. Uncle Elmer told me how they want things done for the market. When I had finished baking bread and rolls he took a pan of rolls in to show Aunt Saloma how nice they were. I was glad he was pleased. He was often difficult to please. Now I knew my work was all right with him. He was in such good humor the entire time I was there and he was helpful. He butchered a hog for market and brought a big slab of meat in for me to cook for dinner. The children said he did it because I was there. They were overjoyed for the meat, not only for themselves but they were glad to share with me. By then I was feeling guilty about the way I felt about coming. The children were so happy to have me there that I was glad to be there.

Saturday Uncle Elmer went to market early. It was clean up time for me. The house wasn't big, but market preparations made a big mess. By evening I had the house clean, the children fed and the supper cleaned away again. The day's work was done and I was tired but I had a feeling of satisfaction that I was able to accomplish all the work I had feared I could not manage. I had the little ones in bed when Uncle Elmer came home from market at 10:00 p.m. His good mood and hearty comment about the clean house made it worth being tired.

The next day after washing the dinner dishes, I played with the children in the living room where Aunt Saloma was. She was feeling much better and laughed along with everyone as we played. The children loved this attention. They didn't often get attention from outside the family. We played, "I Spy" and guessing games. We also made a dummy, dressed him like an old man and sat him on a trunk against the wall. What hilarity they had as they worked on him. I was glad I could share in their pleasure.

Aunt Saloma thought she was well enough to get along all right now so mid-afternoon Noah took me home again. I went home feeling good about the experience. I was the one who had been blessed the most.

After hymn sing one Sunday night four of us girls in the area where I lived had no way home because the boys in the area had other plans before coming home. One of the boys offered his horse and buggy to us girls. Then the boys would come later in one of the other buggies. The buggy we used was an open seated buggy and we all had to crowd on, two girls on the seat and the other two girls on their laps. I drove because no one else wanted to. When we passed a lane that was familiar to the horse, he wanted to turn in. I pulled the left line but saw that won't work, as we would end in the ditch. I quickly pulled the right line again to allow the horse to go into the lane. The horse did not slow down and we made a sharp turn too fast. It caused me to lean far to the left. I was sitting on one of the girls' lap. I had nothing to hang onto except the lines. Since I had pulled the right line and was hanging onto it to get my balance the horse continued to turn to the right after he was in the lane. He turned right into the bean patch in the people's garden. Quickly I pulled the left line. The horse was still running and turned sharply to the left. Now I almost flew out to the right.

We finally got straightened out when we got back into the lane. I allowed the horse to go clear in behind the house where I could circle the horse around with plenty of room to spare. We went back out the lane without stopping. We had a good laugh with that episode but I felt bad about the bean patch. I don't think much harm was done. The girl whose lap I sat on said she could hardly keep me from flying out as she held tightly onto me.

I said, "So that's why I didn't fly out. I kept wondering what's keeping me from flying." I had felt that I had no control since I had only the lines to hold onto. This was the same place, same ditch along the road where my sister Lydia and I were when the line broke. This time the house was dark, indicating everyone was in bed so we didn't stop to apologize. I should have made an attempt to apologize later, but I didn't.

Sometimes when the work was done in the evenings we girls would take the Sunday School Hymnal and sing. Dad would sit and listen. He seemed to enjoy that but looked like he felt sad too. I'm sure memories of Mom came alive, causing a certain sense of loneliness. She used to sing. Sometimes I wonder how it is that a person can have joy and sadness at the same time. The peace and joy one feels when singing the songs is soothing to the heart because of the nearness of God. His love and caring can be felt.

Frequently on Saturday nights when the older boys were finished outdoors and not ready to go to bed yet, they stayed up with us girls while we finished the bits of mending or ironing clothes for church. We had pleasant times together, sometimes with hilarious laughter. Dad joined in our fun. The younger children had had their bathes and were in bed, the house had its weekend cleaning and now it was time for relaxing, even though we were still finishing up some work. It made the work lighter to have the boys and Dad there with us. On nights the boys were tired and went to bed earlier, we girls still enjoyed this time together with Dad. He would not go to bed nights before we did. He lay on the living room floor and slept until we finished our work and went to bed. This is how he used to do with Mom. If there was anything he could help her with he did, but if not, he lay on the floor close by her as she worked.

Dad went to visit his relatives. They lived in North Western, Pennsylvania. He also went to see his friends in Virginia on the same trip. He was away about ten days. Lydia, Bertha and I kept things going at home. The boys did the chores. Fall work was done so they only had school and chores to do.

Uncle Amos and Aunt Mollie and family still came to visit us sometimes and we went to visit them. We always enjoyed them. When they came, the children always wanted to go down the railroad to the river. The river was the main attraction at our place. We loved it as well. It was wooded at the railroad bridge and back away from the fields. It was a pleasant place to be in the summer.

Late in the summer Uncle Amos announced to Dad that they plan to move to Virginia. They made a trip to see about a place to move onto. They planned to move into a tenement house and work for a farmer. This was sad news for us. We would miss them. They planned to have a public auction to sell all of their farm machinery and animals. They wanted a food stand at the auction. They said if we girls would come and help prepare the food and be responsible for selling it at the sale we would get half of the money from the food sales. That was the only exciting thing about their move. We felt like crying when they left. It felt like we would never see them again.

They moved so far away. However, we did see them again.

Winter came and Dad's sister Lizzie was getting married. They lived far from us since we moved to Kenton and then to Branford. We had to start early in the morning to get to the wedding by 9 a.m. There was some snow on the ground. It was an exciting day. First we had the wedding, then the reception that was held in Grandfather Lee's big house. It was an all-day affair, lasting until late at night. Friends and relatives were invited for the noon meal. After dinner the married folks sang hymns appropriate for the occasion. Then there was visiting until supper. After the married folks had supper, all the youth from all the district churches had supper. Then they sang hymns for an hour or more. By then it was late but since this was Dad's sister that got married, we stayed awhile yet. Aunt Lizzie would now live in Pennsylvania with her husband Enos Peachey.

When we left for home it had snowed again and the snow was deep enough to make traveling hard for the horse. Dad stopped every little while to allow the horse to rest. Thankfully it was not so very cold. We were all tired and we all slept on the way home. Dad slept too whenever he stopped to let the horse rest.

In late winter Lydia went to Uncle Eli and Aunt Fannie to help out in western Pennsylvania. She was to stay a month or so. Soon Bertha left to work for Uncle Elam and Aunt Florence. That left me alone with the housework at home. There had been times also when Lydia was alone while Bertha and I worked for someone.

Dad said we three girls could have a setting hen to hatch chicks and then we may have the chicks to sell for money. The cluck was set with the eggs. We needed to sprinkle the eggs every day with water because the cluck was kept inside and could not go out in the morning dew to scratch for food and get her underside wet from the dew. If she were outside she would dampen the eggs herself with that dew.

In early April the chicks began to hatch. I repaired an old coop to put them and the cluck into when they were all hatched. It was a good hatch and I was delighted with them. Lydia and Bertha were still working away so I took care of them.

Dad was also getting the chicken house ready for a new batch of chicks. We cleaned and disinfected the house and put clean sawdust on the floor. The chicken house wasn't quite ready when it was time for Dad to go pick up Lydia in western Pennsylvania. After visiting with his sister and brother-in-law there, Dad and Lydia would go to New Wilmington, Pennsylvania. Dad was getting married April 9, 1946, to a widow, Lavina Mast. She had three children. Mollie, the oldest was near Betty's age, David was near Simon's age and the youngest, Lizzie, was three.

After Dad left, we children continued with the work for the chicks. Edwin and I stretched new feedbags across the windows and fastened them. We spread the clean sawdust, then spread newspaper over the sawdust in a 10-foot diameter under the two stoves so the chicks don't eat the sawdust. Next we had to set up the band of cardboard circling each stove along the edge of the newspaper so that the chicks have to stay close to the stove. They had to stay within its heat. We had a thermometer to check for proper heat. We must not let the heat drop or get too warm. There was a thermostat on the heating stove. That helped us keep the heat even.

A few days after Dad left, the chicks came. I did not go out to help until the deliveryman left. I had a sore foot. New shoes had caused blisters and they got infected. Then, "proud flesh," developed. It was getting better but I still couldn't wear shoes on that foot. I tore strips of cloth from old clothes and wrapped them over the bandages that were on my foot. I did not want the man to see me like that.

When the deliveryman left I went out to take care of them. It was exciting to take care of those little chicks. They had to be taken out of their box and put within the circle. We had clean fresh water in clean jars that were topped with watering trays. Quickly, so the water doesn't splash, we set the jars upside down. This way the jars rested on their trays. The trays only allowed the water down slowly as it was needed. It was lovely to see 500 chicks, so tiny, like fluffy yellow balls with their bright beady black eyes scampering around. The other stove also had 500 chicks.

We needed to see that all the chicks got a drink of water. If they didn't, we took them and put their beaks into the water so they could learn to drink. Many of them went to the water to see what it is all about. They pecked at the water and that way they learned to drink by themselves. Others needed help.

We also set the small feed troughs in the circle for the chicks. We scattered finely cracked corn on the paper. Every few days we put clean paper down. Every day we cleaned the water jars and trays and gave them clean, fresh water.

The fire also had to be kept going. Dad said if I ran out of coal I should go to town and get some. Coal was scarce because of WWII and often we could only get a little at a time in town.

When there was only enough coal for a day or two, I went to the coal yard. They said they are out of coal. I asked, "When will you get more?" They just stood there looking at me. Finally, one said, "I don't know." I asked, "What am I going to do for coal?" They just stood looking at me as though they could not care less.

I went home discouraged. We had to have coal. The train always dropped a little coal along the railroad as it went through, but we had already picked that up. I decided we would go further down the tracks and gather coal for night use. During the day I would keep the fire going with wood. Dad had sometimes burned wood along with the coal to save the coal. Burning wood meant I had to fire the stoves up more often. Dad would be gone two to three weeks and only half that time had passed by the time we were running out of coal. I would be glad when Dad came home to take over the responsibility of dealing with the coal shortage. It took the boys a long time to pick up coal when they had to go so far along the railroad. Then they had such a long distance to carry the heavy loads.

One day I noticed signs of coccidiosis disease in the chicks. We had medicine for that so I gave it to them in their water right away before the case gets so bad. It soon cleared up and by the time Dad came home the chicks looked perky and were growing nicely.

I tried to spring clean the whole house before Dad came home with his new wife. I didn't get the kitchen and living room done in time. A truck came with stepmother's furniture and a message that I was to store it in the small front room. The furniture filled it.

4 LIFE WITH OUR EXPANDED FAMILY

Adjusting to New Family Members
When Dad brought the new family it seemed strange to have another family living with us. This was not just for a while. They were not just visiting and then would leave again. It was permanent. I wasn't sure that I liked it. It was a big adjustment. I am sure they felt the strangeness just a keenly and the adjustment was just as big for them. By the next night I decided I might as well accept it and make the best of it. Once I made that decision I felt better and things fell into place better.

I soon learned to love the children. I always had a soft spot for children. David was Simon's age. Neither had a brother close to his own age before. Now they enjoyed each other's companionship. David didn't talk much, but he laughed a lot. I loved to hear him laugh.

I was sent to town with Lizzie to get her a pair of shoes. During the war it was hard to get shoes like we needed. All I could find was a pair of black shoes with patent leather tips. Lizzie was happy with the shiny black tips on her shoes.

Late in the summer stepsister Mollie became sick with Rocky Mountain spotted fever. She was admitted to the hospital. We did not know if her life would be spared. She pulled through. Sister Betty had the tick fever the next summer. She was in the hospital but didn't get as sick as Mollie had. We recognized the symptoms and took her to the doctor sooner and there was new, better medicine. We were all given shots for this tick fever when Betty got sick.

Aunt Mollie came to see Grandfather Bylers. She came to see us too. How happy we were to see her. Now that there were two more girls added to our family, Lydia slept in the spare bedroom.

Aunt Mollie would sleep with Lydia. Since Aunt Mollie would be leaving already the next day, Bertha and I wanted to be with her too. Aunt Mollie suggested all four of us sleep in one bed. We did. We talked nearly all night. There was so much to catch up on. It was almost like one's mother coming home. It was such a pleasure to have her and was hard to see her leave so soon.

In the fall, my stepmother's parents came for a week's visit. Later one of her sisters and her husband came to visit. They also stayed most of a week. They were all nice people. The sister and husband were especially jolly and happy. My stepmother could be fun too when she felt well.

We had lots of snow while they were with us. I wore Dad's tall boots to hang up clothes. It wasn't so cold anymore but the snow was deep and made it hard to hang the clothes. Sheets and other large articles wanted to hang down on top of the snow. My brothers shoveled paths along the clothesline. I enjoyed being out in the snow. This visiting step-uncle helped me get the clothes hung. He was so jolly it made the chore fun.

I was also working away when Enos was born to Dad and Stepmother on February 12, 1947. Now I had a new brother and came home to help with the housework. When I looked at him in the crib, my heart went out to him with love. I had had mixed feelings about this baby joining our family, but once I saw him, all that changed. I was the one responsible for his care since his mom was sick for a long time. After she was up and around she still was not strong. I greatly enjoyed baby Enos. We loved each other.

Lydia was working for Uncle John and Aunt Mary. We did not see her often anymore. She was in another church district and quite a distance away.

In March, eleven and one-half months after Dad's wedding, Lydia married Freeman Coblentz from Ohio. Two days before the wedding I baked the cakes. The special cake was larger than the rest. It was a coconut cake and was considered the wedding cake, to be served to the bride and groom, the attendants and those who cooked and served the meals. The day before the wedding the pies for one of the meals were made. Other foods were also prepared. Wedding receptions took a lot of food, as it was an all-day affair. We had chicken, dressing, mashed potatoes and all the trimmings.

After the wedding Lydia moved to Ohio with Freeman. I missed her a lot and wondered when I would get to see her again. Ohio seemed so far away. They did come to see us early in the fall. How glad I was to see her. We all were. They stayed several days

In the summer Dad took Stepmother to see her family in Pennsylvania. They took all of her children along. I sewed clothes for them before they left. Little Enos grew so fast I needed to make him a good many clothes.

My parents planned to be gone two weeks. Bertha and I had plenty to do while they were gone. We took care of the garden and canned 100 or more quarts of peaches. I also made some clothes for the boys and we had mending to do. We also had the regular chores and cooking to do. We got a lot of work done in the two weeks they were gone, but not as much as I had hoped to do.

One Sunday while they were gone Uncle Andy and Aunt Eva came to visit. They lived about 40 miles south and we didn't get to see them often. They came after lunch and had supper with us. They brought hoagies for the supper. Another day Grandfather Bylers came to visit. It was so special to have Uncle Andys and Grandfather Bylers come. They were such dear people in my life.

All the youth from church planned a picnic at Silver Lake, about two miles from our house. We roasted hotdogs and had other good food. The boys fished while the girls set the food up. A few of the boys built a fire for roasting hot dogs. Ira Nissley asked me to stick a hotdog on his roasting stick. I wondered why.

We enjoyed the whole afternoon by that river. It was a lovely place in a wooded area with lots of large rocks. At 4 p.m. it was time for everyone to leave the peaceful scene and go home to tend to chores. A few months later, Ira Nissley asked me for a date and I accepted.

When Dad's came home they said they plan to move to Pennsylvania. What a shock that was. Meeting strangers was a trial for me and if I went to Pennsylvania I wouldn't know anyone. I just can't. I didn't know what to do. My mind went around and around. I would think of each of my brothers and sisters, first one and then another. How could I see them go and I stay behind? And Dad! I would miss them so. How can I disappoint Dad? I must go with them, but I can't.

I did not go. Ira wanted us to get married. That made it easier to stay. My family left late in Nov. I felt sick when they left, but I knew that when we go to my parents' home for our wedding I would see them again.

When my family left I stayed with Grandfather Bylers until my wedding. When my family moved, they had a sale of the things they did not take with them. I asked Grandfather to bid on the little white dresser Dad had purchased for us girls' bedroom when we were still all at home. Now those days were over. I bought the dresser for three dollars and was happy to have something from home.

5 MARRIAGE AND CHILDREN

Setting Up House

Ira had his 21st birthday on February 10, 1948. I had turned 20 in October. We felt we were old enough and went to PA so we could be married at my parents' home. Ira's Dad was a bishop in the church. He, Ira's mother, one of Ira's brothers, and one sister came to our wedding. He married us on February 22, 1948!

We stayed with my parents for a few weeks. We made one quilt and one comforter for our own home. When we left my parents, we went to see sister Lydia and Freeman in Ohio. Her first child had just been born. We stayed four days, then went back to Delaware, where we stayed with Ira's parents until we had our own home ready.

We rented a duplex from Daniel Miller and his wife Liza. They lived in the other part. We had two rooms upstairs and two rooms

downstairs. I was eager to get everything fixed
up, but I got sick with the flu the second day
after we came home. I was quite sick for a few
days. Thursday I got up for a little while.
Friday I wanted to go with Ira to the Farmers
Market and Auction to purchase produce and
things for our new home. Now I was too sick.
My mother-in-law went with Ira to help him
know the most needed things to get to start
housekeeping. I already had a bed my parents
gave, and the little white dresser. I also had a
chest of drawers Grandfather Bylers loaned us.

At the auction Ira bought a small drop-
leaf table, four wooden folding chairs, and a
kitchen cabinet. His mother bought a box with
an assortment of china plates, cups, saucers,
glasses, and other items. There were enough to
set the dinner table for everyday use. We could
save the nice china table settings my brothers
and sisters gave us for wedding gifts for
company dinners. Ira's mother also gave us
stainless steel flatware, a fry pan, two
saucepans, a kerosene lamp, a broom, a
dustpan, a bucket and two dishpans.

Ira's parents had bought a new kerosene
cook stove. We fixed up the old one and
painted it. It looked almost new. They also had
a new sewing machine and we borrowed the
old one. I gave the sewing machine cabinet a

coat of varnish. I cleaned and painted the kitchen cabinet white. Ira put new hinges and latches on it. That made the cabinet look nearly new. I also cleaned and varnished the chairs. Ira's parents also gave us a cow and one dozen laying hens.

We borrowed a wagon from Ira's Dad and hitched two horses to the wagon. We loaded all our belongings to the wagon, including a chicken coop with our hens. We tied the cow to the back of the wagon, but she refused to follow us. We could not go like this if she would not walk. We couldn't just drag her. I took up the lines and drove the horses while Ira stayed with the cow and brought her along. We had four miles to go. There wasn't much to unload and we soon had our few belongings unloaded.

There was a built-in cupboard in the house and a built-in cabinet, but no sink. I set the dishpans on top of the counter and was careful not to splash water out of the pans. We had stayed with Ira's parents about six weeks. When we moved it was the beginning of April and sunny and warm. We did get a few cool days. We borrowed a small tin heater to use on those days. We were cozy and happy to be in our own home.

I enjoyed keeping my own house, yet at first it felt more like I am playing at housekeeping. Ira did carpenter work with Daniel Miller. Ira grew up on a farm, but he preferred carpentry.

Since we had invited only a few people to our wedding we did not get as many gifts as couples usually received. However, relatives and friends had given us linens and some cookware at our wedding and we had the gifts from our parents and the things from the auction. We were happy for those things and with Ira's paychecks we were able to get the other things we needed.

Every Saturday we went to town to get groceries. When we were ready to start home, Ira would buy us each a pint of ice cream to eat on the way home. I had seldom had ice cream, except when someone made it. It was such a treat to eat this store ice cream in the buggy on the way home with my new husband. I usually could not finish my whole pint but Ira gladly finished it for me. Ira was tall and thin. I was much shorter, but also thin. We could use a little extra weight so the ice cream did not hurt us.

Every week I went to Grandpa Bylers to do laundry. I also did Grandpa and Grandma's laundry while there. One week I arrived at

Grandpa's and their rose bush was covered with lovely, delicate, pink roses. Mom had given this rose bush to Grandma. Grandma greatly cherished it, especially now that Mom was so missed. I was glad Mom had been able to give it to her.

We had bought a small pig, butchered and canned it. This gave us meat and in the summer we planted a garden and I canned vegetables. We bought fruit for canning. I was busy all summer, but not as busy as when I had worked for big families or at home with our big family.

That summer we took a trip to Virginia to see Uncle Amos and Aunt Mollie. They had another baby now, nine-month-old Katie. It was so good to see the whole family again. We visited Ira's Uncle Eli and Aunt Saloma in Virginia. Ira's brother Calvin and his wife Lena went along as well as one of Ira's cousins and his wife.

We went to Maryland before returning to Delaware to visit some friends. While there, we went with our friends to the Potomac River. We went out on rowboats. I did not enjoy the boating. The men were too rough and I was afraid. First, some boys rocked our boat, then jumped in and almost upset the boat. Their weight overloaded the boat. Then Ira and

Calvin tied our boat to a motorboat. Lena and I did not want to. The motorboat was large and made a long, wide swell of water out the back. Calvin and Ira wanted to ride on that swell. The motorboat sped up and gave us a fast ride. I was so scared. We learned later that that is against the law. I still don't like boating.

In the late fall we bought a baby crib and I started preparing for the arrival of a baby. I made most of the gowns and everything needed except shirts, diapers and blankets. I was finished sewing the baby's things long before we needed them. Little David Leroy arrived January 26, 1949. Oh, I was so delighted with my baby boy. I was so happy caring for him. He liked having me talk to him and play with him. He was a good baby and I loved him so. It was the same with each child born to us. We called David "Sonny Boy" when he was little.

Grandpa Bylers were visiting in Florida when David was born. Grandfather wanted to come home as soon as he heard the news. He wanted to see our baby.

When David was one month old we went to see my parents in Pennsylvania. We were saving quarters and had almost enough to cover the train fare. Ira dug the rest out of his pocket. At that time, it cost only about 30 dollars. We left David with Ira's parents. They later told us how much they enjoyed him and how much they missed him. However, my Dad was so disappointed that we had left David at home and they didn't get to see him.

When David was six months old Grandpa Bylers decided to move to Virginia to be close to their children. Uncle Amoses, Uncle Adams, and Uncle Johns all lived in the same area of Virginia. Uncle Adam and Uncle John had built houses on adjoining lots in Stuarts Draft, Virginia. They built a small house on Uncle John's lot for Grandpa and Grandma. I felt sad indeed to have them move away. They were the last close relatives of mine in the Dover, Delaware area. I still had a few Uncles and Aunts but most of my cousins weren't grown yet.

Grandma and Grandpa were taking the place of my parents for me as well. They loved me, cared about me and were there for me.

Before they left they had an auction to dispose of the things they were not taking. We were there the day of the sale. I was standing by the kitchen door when Grandma was coming through with a small, light walnut, antique table with white casters. It was a fancy table and she was on her way to put it up for auction. Then she turned to me and said, "Here, I am giving this table to you."

I was surprised and appreciated the gift because it is so typical of her sharing, giving nature. Because of her I still cherish that table.

After David was a year old my sister Bertha and Levi Mast got married. We went to the wedding. This time we took David along.

Two years after our wedding, in February, Ira and I moved to another house. We already knew three of the closest neighbors. That was a comfort. On March 22, 1950, Lydia Irene was born to us. We wrote her name Irene, but mostly called her Rene (Rene pronounced with long e's.) Rene was darker complected, with dark brown eyes and thick, long, black hair. The hospital nurse tied a tiny pink ribbon on to her hair but it barely stayed on. Her hair was hardly long enough to tie the ribbon to.

David's complexion was just the opposite. He was fair with golden blonde curls and large blue eyes. By the time Rene was six months old, her hair turned light brown and was curly too.

In December 1950, we went to Virginia to see Grandpa and Grandma Byler. This time Ira thought we should move to Virginia. Uncle John thought wages would be better there. I had mixed feelings about the move. Ira had a good steady job with the carpenter crew in Delaware. It didn't seem he could do better than that. But, I trusted Ira and we liked Virginia. Still, I did not like leaving Delaware. It was home and everything was familiar. I would miss the people. By now I had learned to know some of the church people in Virginia and also I had more close relatives in Virginia than in Delaware. However, leaving Delaware would mean leaving Ira's family and I would miss them.

Life in Virginia

We moved to the Shenandoah Valley of Virginia in January 1951. I never regretted our move. There are so many good things about Virginia. I never get tired of the hills and the mountains. We settled near the town of Stuarts Draft.

A year later, Linda Katherine was born on March 28, 1952. She too had brown hair and eyes and was so dainty. When she was nine months old we went to see my parents and most of my brothers and sisters in Pennsylvania. We also went to see Freeman and Lydia in Ohio, then on to Bertha and Levi. Bertha and Levi now lived on a farm in New York. Uncle Amos and Aunt Mollie were going and took us along. It was winter and snowed the first night we were in New York. We started home at four the next morning, trying to get out of the snow before we get stranded. It was already slippery in places. We drove carefully and were under considerable suspense until, after many long miles, we left the snow behind us.

September 1953 we rented and moved to the 45-acre Moorhead farm. Paul Daniel was born November 22, 1953. He too, had brown hair and brown eyes. David, Rene, and Linda had measles that winter. Paul didn't get them. Right after the measles they had the chicken pox. Paul had only two pox, but it was enough to make him immune to chicken pox.

We started attending East Bethel church while living here. We joined and went to this church about 12 years. The congregation was renting a building on Avis road when we started going there. They built a new building on a lot on Cold Springs Road, Stuarts Draft, in 1956. Ira laid the bricks.

We enjoyed living on the Moorhead farm. Ira planted corn. To prepare the land for planting, he had to clear the small trees growing scattered on part of a field. He tied a chain around the trunk of these saplings and hooked the other end of the chain to the tractor, one by one. He started the tractor and moved forward, pulling on the tree until it was uprooted. Sometimes the front of the tractor reared up. I was afraid the tractor would rear so high that it would topple over backwards onto him.

On the Moorhead farm we also had a thousand or more chicks. We raised them to sell at broiler size. By the time they were sold, prices had dropped so low, we only broke even. We could not stay when we could not earn money, so we stayed less than a year.

In July 1954 we moved to Staunton. Ira started mason work. He hired a teenager, Lee Strictler, to be his helper. Lee mixed mud and carried brick and block to Ira.

One day when I was washing, Paul was outside the house playing. He could crawl, but could not yet walk. Soon a man came and asked if my baby was on the road. I quickly went to see. What a fright! There sat Paul in the middle of the road! I thought surely that the man would have picked Paul up and brought him in. There wasn't much traffic on the road, but plenty to be dangerous.

In the middle of the next summer the house we were living in sold. We needed to move. We also wanted to start David to school at Augusta Mennonite School, the Christian

Day School of our church. Ira found a piece of land in Fishersville at a reasonable price. The bus would come that far to pick David up. The children went to this school until 1963. The school closed in the mid-sixties.

We had a long street out to the highway where David was to wait for the bus. At the end of the street, along Route 250, was Coffey's Service Station. When it was cold the children waited inside.

That summer of 1955 Ira built a basement, partitioned off rooms and put on a flat roof. The basement was against a slope and the back was walk in, level with the ground. A porch was built onto the backside of the basement. We had a porch swing on it. It was a pleasant place to sit in the evening. We started moving on August 9, 1955. Then we had a surprise. Brenda Joy was born to us that day! We all stayed at Amos Zooks until I was strong enough to go ahead with the work. Aunt Mollie Zook and Aunt Mattie Byler put the furniture in order and cleaned before we moved into the basement.

Brenda had black hair one inch long that stuck straight up. She had large blue eyes. In a month or two her hair lay down and soon was golden blonde and curly. Brenda was afraid of anything black such as the black stovepipe and black-framed glasses. Poor Uncle Amos. He wanted to talk to her and hold her, but she was afraid of his black hair and glasses. She soon outgrew some of her fear, but still had a fear of certain black things.

The summer Brenda turned two, she came in from playing and was fussy. I thought she must be hungry and gave her a cracker. She was still feeling out of sorts, walked out the door and threw the cracker on the ground. She came in and sat on a big chair where she could see out the door. Soon she saw a bird eating her cracker. Then she really cried! The bird was not to have her cracker!

I had an old book that I would draw pictures in on the pages at the end of chapters that were not printed full. I drew a picture of the bird eating Brenda's cracker and gave it to Brenda. After that, when she had the book, she would hunt for that picture of the bird eating her cracker.

One day after church Brenda came running and crying. When she saw me she said she saw a "Yea over black dog" whatever that meant. She explained that it was a big black dog. The dog was in the neighboring yard. In her mind, since the dog was black it was really to be feared.

John Garland was born to us on March 17, 1957. We called him Johnny Boy for several years. He had large blue eyes and brown curly hair. At age one and a half, Ira took him for his first haircut. I asked Ira not to allow the barber to cut off all of his curls on the top of his head. I wanted the hair on top to only be shortened a little. These curls seemed a part of Johnny and I didn't want to lose them. When Ira came home all the curls were gone. The barber had cropped the hair short, almost like a butch haircut. I was devastated. "Oh, my baby," I said, and ran into our bedroom and cried.

When Johnny was six months old, Ira found an advertisement in the newspaper from an art instruction school. It asked interested people to draw a face and send it in. Ira thought I should give it a try. I did. When I got a letter and a form to fill out it requested that I draw a picture of my choice. I did that too. Next they sent a representative to interview me. He explained the course for drawing and painting lessons. We decided to try it. For about a year I could keep up.

Then my life was so busy I had to give it up. I had completed four books of lessons. There were many more to go, but I had gotten the basics of black and white drawing, of color values, watercolor painting and color mixing. Since my books were paid for, the school sent the rest of my books to me. Over the years I continued to study on my own at a much slower pace.

In September 1958, my sister Lydia wrote that she had twin girls, Rosalee and Rhodalee. I was excited about her twins. I had never thought to wish for twins before, but now I wanted twins. I never did have twins.

Timothy Dale was born November 1, 1958. He had light hair and brown eyes. Later his eyes became golden brown with flecks of blue and light green mixed at the outer edges.

From the cradle on, Timmy always looked for challenges. He never could keep up with his brain. He wanted to try everything before he was old enough. Once he could walk he was more content because he could go where he wanted and do what he wanted. When he started walking he walked well and soon ran. He followed the other children out to play.

Tim was not quite two when he climbed on the electric cooking range and sat on a burner. Then he started turning knobs, I came into the kitchen and grabbed him. When I checked, he had red rings on his bottom but was not actually burned yet. I was just in time!

Christmas Memories with Our Children

The year Rene was six and Linda four, for Christmas, we had my grandfather build a dollhouse for them. It was about 12 x 36 inches and had three rooms downstairs and three upstairs. It had a peaked roof. Grandfather was doing it from his wheelchair because of his arthritis. I bought dollhouse furniture for it. After Brenda was born and old enough to help, she and Linda decorated with curtains cut from catalogs and glued to windows, lamps and end tables also from the catalogs glued into place, and with scraps of corduroy for carpet.

The same year we bought a barn and animals Grandfather made for Paul and David. There was a white board fence to set up around the barn for the animals. When John and Tim came along, they rigged up a bailer of sorts and bailed hay. They used grass for hay. They cut and dried it, then stored it in the barn. Once summer they spent many hours with the barn. Then they sort of outgrew the barn or lost interest.

While the children attended Augusta Mennonite School, we enjoyed the yearly Christmas programs so much. When Rene was in the first grade, she learned a few Christmas songs. One was a lullaby. Brenda was one and a half years old and started singing the lullaby. She stood on the seat of the rocker and sang as she rocked. She spent a lot of time rocking this way, chanting phrases of whatever came to her mind and singing this lullaby and parts of other songs.

Before Brenda could talk, when we went anywhere, she would stand on the seat of the car, behind my arm to be safe. She would pat my shoulder and motion for me to sing. If I didn't sing the song she wanted, she would tap my shoulder and say, "No, no." I would start other songs until I had the one she wanted. I knew which songs she liked best, so it was not hard to select the right one after a few tries.

The year Brenda started to school, the first and second grade teacher asked me to draw a manger scene with colored chalk on a sheet. I accepted the challenge, although I had never used chalk in this manner. I spread the sheet out on the floor to work. I decided to have only the manger scene in the picture. I drew an open doorway. It was dark inside except where the light shone on Mary. She sat holding baby Jesus in her arms behind the manger. Joseph was at her side. With this much space, I painted them life size. I was happy with my chalk drawing, perhaps because I had accomplished a difficult task. At the Christmas program, the sheet was hung on the wall. Then the children representing the ones in the birth story, came to see Jesus.

Another Christmas, when Steve was three years old, we did not have money for Christmas presents. We had some left over lumber still in the basement. I had had some experience working with wood soon after we married. I had taken scraps of wood and made a little doll cradle. It looked a little crude, but with some fabric I had I made a rag doll and clothes for the doll. This went in the cradle so little girls would have something to play with when they came to visit.

Now, for Christmas I began leafing through magazines for ideas. I found handmade platypus and raccoon benches. That was a good idea for John, Tim and Steve. Then I saw boxes decorated by decoupage. That would be just the thing for the girls, but what could I give David and Paul. I'll think about it as I work, I thought.

Borrowing my Uncle Adam's jigsaw, I got started building. First I drew the sides of raccoons on paper. Then I drew the head and back ends that formed the tails. Instead of making the seats solid, I formed a box with a lid to serve as a storage place. I did the same with Steve's platypus. I transferred the patterns onto the wood and cut them out with the jigsaw and nailed them together. I bought small cans of paint at 35 cents a can. I painted the raccoons green with black faces, tails, and feet. I made the platypus light blue with a yellow beak and feet. His eyes were black with white.

Next I made the boxes for the girls. They were ten inches square. I got them cut, nailed together and painted pink. I had no time left for decoupage. Later I painted them gold, then decoupaged clusters of flowers from wallpaper to match the boxes.

A few days later our closest neighbor, Mrs. Warren had come to visit and gave me ten dollars for Christmas money. I bought David and Paul each a billfold and put a dollar bill into each. I got a hanky to put in the girls' boxes. I got a paddle with a ball on a rubber band attached to put in the younger boys' bench boxes. I also got an orange and a little candy for each of the children. They were happy with their gifts. I thought it was better than nothing at all.

This same year, the school decided that instead of having the school children exchange names and give gifts to each other, each family would prepare a Christmas package for children in other countries. We did not have the money to buy the clothes and things required for this. Mrs. Warren bought them for us. God bless her!

Living in the House We Built

The winter of 1959 through the spring of 1960 we had a lot of snow. There were many days Ira could not go to work because of this snow so we thought it would be a good time to build our house. We were still living in the basement. After we had the trim on, I did the sanding, painting, wood fillers and varnishing. The living room and bedroom floors were varnished. The rest of the floors were vinyl tiles or linoleum. I laid them out in a pattern.

Grandfather Byler died early May 1960. Even though the house wasn't finished we quickly moved upstairs before the funeral. We knew family from out of state would be coming and need places to stay. By moving we could use the extra bedrooms.

Grandfather had been sick for a few months. He had been in a wheel chair for a number of years because of arthritis. Then he developed cancer and became sick fast. His last three weeks of life he did not eat. He suffered so much. He was so thin his body looked like only skin and bones. For his sake we were glad when he died. In all his years of suffering from arthritis he remained cheerful, kind, and loving. We greatly missed him. Now Grandma lived alone. There were lonely days for her, but she was brave and had a smile for everyone. We often stopped to see her.

In the summer of 1960 we went to see our families. We all piled in the car. We went to Pennsylvania to see my parents and married brothers and sisters. Then we went to see Freeman and Lydia in Canada. This was the first time we visited them in Canada. We also visited Ira's brother and sisters in other parts of Canada. Then we went on to New York to see Bertha and her family.

Soon after we came home from our trip my Grandfather Lee in Meyersdale, Pennsylvania died. We had a problem finding the church building where the funeral was. We did not arrive until the service was over. At the graveside they opened the casket again so we could see Grandfather. Dad was there but my stepmother did not come. My sister Lydia and Freeman were there. I saw a lot of friends and relatives I had not seen in a long time.

When I was little and we went to visit Grandpa Lees he was out working, so I saw more of Grandma and the aunts. By the time I was seven years old, Grandpa had a sore leg that did not heal for many years. He was always sitting in a rocking chair with his leg wrapped in bandages and resting up on a chair. He could still get around some but could not work much. There were usually a lot of visitors there at the same time so I never learned to know Grandpa Lee as well.

Late in the summer we went to see Ira's family in Delaware. We also visited Uncle Clarence and Aunt Sylvia who still lived in Delaware. I felt we did a lot of traveling that summer. It was so good to see so many of the family and relatives.

Three or four weeks before our new baby, Steve was born, Ira's sister, Ella, in Canada died. I could not go, but said that Ira should go. I had just been sick in bed with kidney infection and my strength was slow coming back. The day that he left Ira picked a few lima beans that were still on the vines. I sat shelling the beans when I heard John and Tim down on the basement porch. I thought that as long as I could hear them they would be all right. Tim was almost three and John was four. They needed to be watched all the time.

Tim was always getting into mischief and John was always with him, watching, sometimes helping. Where one was the other was.

After a while I did not hear the boys but I was so weak and tired. It was about time for the children to come home from school. I would send them to check on the boys. When they walked in the door they noticed the boys weren't around. Rene asked, "Where are the little boys."

"I don't know," I said. "Quick, go look for them. I last heard them down on the basement porch."

David went down there to see. He looked everywhere and was soon back. He said, "I can't find them. Aren't they in here?"

"No," I said, beginning to be alarmed. The other children were searching too. I said, "Don't look in here. I know they are outdoors."

David made a quick search of the house and went back out onto the basement porch again. This time he heard a very faint cry. He opened the old refrigerator door. Johnny and Timmy came tumbling out, dripping wet. David brought them into the dining room where I sat. They were still crying. I cried, "Johnny and Timmy," and held out my hands to them. They each laid their head on one of my knees and cried. David told me where they were. He said they could hardly cry anymore. He said there was a puddle of water in the bottom of the refrigerator because of condensation. I asked for a towel and dried their faces and hair, took off their clothes and dried them all over. I dressed them again with dry clothes.

Then they told me what they did. Ira had the old, worn out refrigerator filled with tools. They took out all the tools, then crawled in. The door shut itself. They could not get out. They were in there about 10 minutes. If the refrigerator gasket around the door had been totally tight, they probably would not have lived. It is only by the grace of God that they are still alive.

After Ira came home I told him the story. He said that when they had gone to bed that night, Uncle Mose prayed that "our families would be kept safe from harm". Ira told me he had felt that wasn't necessary, that we were going to be okay. "Now I see it differently," Ira said. "They must have been saved for a purpose." It was a very bad experience for the boys and a bad experience for me.

November 2, 1961 our family was completed when Steven Eugene was born. He had black hair and dark brown eyes. Since he was so much younger than the other boys and quieter natured, he spent a lot of contented hours playing alone with his toys or in his high chair. He liked to sit in the high chair and sort objects, such as buttons, organizing them into sets based on color, item type or size. Buttons, small toys, cars, whatever he could make collections and sets of, brought him hours of fun. Sometimes we heard him play auction with his rows of things. When he played outside it was usually with Linda. When he was old enough to ride bicycle or enter other activities with the older boys he would play with them.

One day Steve needed air in his bike tire. John went with him to Coffeys to help him put the air in the tire. On the way back home John rode ahead and did not see Stevie fly off his bicycle. Soon Ira came down the street and saw a boy lying on the street. It was almost dark. Ira got out of the car and checked to see whom it was and why he didn't get up. Then he saw it was Steve and brought him to the house. He guided him through the door. "Help Steve," he said to me. "I found him lying on the road beside his bicycle." Then Ira went back out and Steve sat on a chair opposite of where I sat shelling beans.

"What happened?" I asked. He didn't answer. He kept his eyes closed. I saw he was not acting as he normally did. I carried him to the couch and laid him down. He answered no questions. He had scratches down the front under his shirt and black oil from the road. I asked the other boys what happened but they didn't know. John explained how he had gone with Steve to get air in his tire but on the way back, once on our street, he had biked ahead of Steve and didn't see what happened.

I got warm water to clean him up but he kept trying to sit up and asking, "Where is my bike? I need to ride my bike." I didn't allow him to sit up. Although he talked, he talked only about his bike. His eyes looked strange and confused. We took him to the hospital emergency room. They x-rayed and found a skull fracture. The fracture was in the crosspiece bone in the temple. They kept him at the hospital for four days until the doctor could see he was acting normal again. At first he slept most of the time and didn't talk. When he did talk a little he would ask things like, "Where am I? Why are all those bars there? When we answered he forgot right away and didn't know he asked. Not until the fourth day did he remember anything. He never did remember the accident.

A few years later, we had to take Tim to the hospital. He had rammed a barn-fork through his foot. Ira could not get the fork out and we had to take him to the hospital with the fork still stuck through his foot. The doctor numbed Tim's foot and worked hard to get the fork out. They kept Tim in the hospital a few days to watch for infection and give him shots of antibiotics. They wrapped wet towels of Epsom salt around his foot and kept it warm with a heating pad. Tim had fun with the nurses. They kept popping in and out of his room just to tease with him. They brought him ice cream and anything he wanted. They spoiled him, which certainly delighted Tim.

Tim had other accidents while growing up. When he was four years old David was boiling milk to feed the calves. Just as David took the milk off the stove, Tim came running through the kitchen and ran against the pan of milk. The milk spilled on Tim's chest, scalding him. I wasn't home. Rene got the neighbor lady to take her and Tim to the doctor. I felt guilty for having been away all day. Tim had little pain after the doctor sprayed it with Vaseline. Later the doctor told me that by sealing the air off the pain stops. I was to keep the burn covered with Vaseline at all times until it healed. It did heal nicely with no scabs developing, but it left ridges of bright pink scars.

A few years later, we started taking Vitamins A, D, E, and C. After some months, the ridges disappeared. Ever since then I have used Vitamin E squeezed directly out of a capsule onto the burns instead of Vaseline. I have wonderful results this way, with no scars or scabs.

When Tim was twelve, Ira asked him to pour gasoline in the carburetor of the car while Ira pumped the accelerator. The car backfired. It splashed gasoline from the carburetor into Tim's face and caught fire instantly. Tim ran. Because the hood was up Ira did not see what happened until Tim ran away from the car. Ira hollered loudly for him to stop as he ran after Tim.

When I heard the holler I ran to the window to see what was the matter. I could see nothing. I waited a moment. In the meantime, Tim found a water hole behind the haystack. He stuck his head in the water and had all the fire out except the back of his head. Ira caught up with him and put out the remaining fire. Then I saw them walking from the haystack. I could not see what was wrong, but I could tell from the slumped way they walked with their heads down that something was wrong. I ran out. When I met them, they told me what had happened as we continued to the house. Right away I poured vitamin E oil on all areas of the burns. The skin was burned white, especially his ear. His hair was mostly singed off in the back, but his scalp was not burned. Before I finished putting on the vitamin E, Ira went back outside. Then Tim turned white as a sheet and sat limply in the chair he had been sitting in. I ran out and called Ira to come quick and help. "We need to take him to the doctor! He has gone into shock!"

The doctor sent us to the emergency room and called the burn specialist. Tim said by the time we got to the hospital the pain was gone. Vitamin E took the pain away. He was admitted to the hospital. The nurses kept asking if it hurt, but Tim insisted it did not. They could not understand why it didn't hurt. They said, "If it starts to hurt, let us know. We have something to give you." It was never necessary.

Three or four days later Tim was allowed to go home. The doctor gave some cream we were to keep putting on. They showed Tim how to do it. They said, "There is no reason your mom should have to do this." Tim always did it himself. The second day after coming home Tim's face was swollen as big as with the mumps. The doctor prescribed a different ointment and the swelling went down.

When we brought Tim home I asked the doctor if I could put Vitamin E on the burns. He said, "Lady, you leave my burn alone and say no more." I did not put Vitamin E on, but I gave him plenty by mouth. When Tim went back for a checkup, the doctor expressed amazement at how nice his skin looked. Tim had no scars. The doctor said he had expected Tim's ear to be deformed but it was normal. Only if Tim was excited or flushed did his ear get a little pinker than the rest of his skin. Finally, even that sign of his burn disappeared. I did not tell the doctor that Tim's first treatment was Vitamin E and that he had taken plenty by mouth through the healing at home. How thankful I was that it healed so nicely.

John had problems with poison ivy. The poison grew along the fence by the gates where the boys took the cows through to the 50-acre pasture and an old apple orchard we rented. The calves grazed all through the orchard and the pasture. In the summer time John broke out with poison many times. Nothing helped much but medicated foam the doctor prescribed.

John and Tim had what they called their pet calves. When the calves were older, they started riding them to pasture. The boys often roamed the pasture and orchard. There was a small pond in the pasture. In the winter it froze deep enough to skate. We did not have skates but skated with our shoes.

Sometimes on Sunday afternoons we would all go for a walk up the pasture to the orchard. We picked wild flowers. Sometimes we went across Route 250 to a neighboring pond. Summers and after school in the spring and fall, Paul, John and Tim went fishing at this pond. They caught mostly bluegills and sunfish. They were small fish, but the boys cleaned them and cut off their heads. I fried them whole. They were good. Sometimes they went to a pond a few miles away. They always walked. John was not as interested in fishing as Paul and Tim and did not always go along.

The boys also enjoyed frog gigging. This needed to be done after dark. They skinned the legs, cleaned them and then I would fry them. As they fried, the legs jumped and kicked around, so I did not like to fry them. The boys started frying their own frog legs. They did not mind and only laughed at the jumping legs. We knew the jumps were only reflex nerves and the frogs could not be hurting now.

One summer we planned a picnic to Ramsey's Camp. Ira was selling real estate and his boss, Mr. Ramsey, offered us the use of his camp. It was set back in a quiet woods.

After much planning and fixing a picnic lunch, we started for the camp after church service. "We're going to Ramsey's Camp. We're going to Ramsey's Camp," the younger children chanted in the back seat. "Will you boys be quiet?" said Rene. "This doesn't call for such a noise." Nevertheless, she was as excited as the rest of us. We had never had a family outing just like this and we all thought it was great.

After traveling for about 30 minutes we began to wonder if we had taken a wrong turn. This road was narrow and not traveled much. We kept going and after a few minutes we came around a curve and there it was on a sign above the gate in large letters we read, "The Hiding Place".

"This is it," said Ira. There were about two acres of cleared land with a cabin and an outdoor fireplace. It was really a kitchen cook stove set into a brick jacket, leaving the front and top exposed. There was a fishpond. The boys had their fishing poles and started digging for worms. The ground was so dry they couldn't find any. They threw their hooks into the water. "Look, I caught a fish already," said Paul. "The fish are so hungry they grab for the hook without a worm." The fish were so small that the boys threw back whatever they caught.

Soon the boys tired of fishing and decided it would be more fun to ride the old rowboat. They soon got in it and started rowing. It leaked and required dipping out the water. They didn't mind. Every little while they had to dip more water.

Rene and I worked at getting a fire hot enough to roast hot dogs and heat soup. The stove was stubborn and took some coaxing. Ira took this chance for a nap on a blanket. He worked hard all week and liked to rest on Sundays.

When the lunch was ready the children thought it a great treat. They didn't often get hot dogs so the dogs were special. So was the coconut pie. I didn't often make it.

After lunch was cleared away, Rene decided she wanted to row the boat. She and Linda got in and started out. They inched their way out, trying to use the oars. When Rene got out a ways and wanted to come back, she couldn't turn the boat. She called to David for help. He waded out and turned the boat. Then she rowed in. Too soon it was time to leave. It had been a beautiful day. A sense of quiet peace at the place seemed to become part of all of us. We were a quieter bunch going home. Soon the little ones fell asleep.

The summer Steve was four, we all packed into the station wagon and went visiting most of our family again. We traveled to several parts of Pennsylvania where we visited my parents and most of my brothers and sisters. We also visited Ira's parents and brothers and sisters who lived in Pennsylvania. By that time most of Ira's family had left Delaware. From there we went on to New York to see Bertha and her family, then to Canada to see Ira's sisters and brother. Last we went to see my sister Lydia and family near Kitchener, Canada. Their children and ours were all near the same age. We stayed three days. The children and all of us had so much fun together. It was the same way when we went to Ira's brother Clemens and family. Their children were also the ages of our children and they had so much fun.

When we traveled like that we took lots of blankets and pillows along. We spread them in the back of the station wagon and the four younger children sat or lay back there on the blankets as they pleased. When they got tired they slept. When we stayed at someone's house overnight we took the blankets and pillows in to make pallets on the floor. The

families could not have beds for all of us.
Sometimes there was a bed for Ira and me. If
not, we slept on the floor with the children.

We enjoyed that trip so much. We tried
to make the most of it, not expecting to be able
to take all of the children along again. As the
younger ones grew, the family would not all fit
in the station wagon and mini-vans did not
exist. I am so glad we made that trip. We all
enjoyed it so much and it was indeed the last
trip we took with all the children along.

In 1967 Ira decided it was better for us to
home school. We needed to file papers in the
county superintendent's office to remove them
from public school. We got books from the
county at a low price. Steve wanted to start
school too, even though he was only five. I
thought he could try. He did well and
continued first grade through to the end of the
year. He passed and was ready for the second
grade. Rene taught the first year and I taught
thereafter. David had graduated from high
school the year before. Rene went to live with
and assist Lil Pennell. Lil was a quadriplegic
and needed help at home. Lil worked as a
counselor and had a doctorate in education.
When Rene wanted to finish her high school,
the school allowed Lil to tutor Rene in the last
two classes she needed. Rene was happy to get

her diploma from her own school, Wilson Memorial.

After teaching school a few years, I felt I need to learn what John and Tim had in their math books so I could teach them. I started attending the Adult Learning Center. I even got my GED diploma and later worked there as a teacher assistant. That gave me a feeling of accomplishment.

I had three domesticated mallard ducks. They usually walked in single file. The boys dug a little pond with the tractor and scoop. The ducks enjoyed their pond immensely. Before the boys made the pond the ducks had used the cows watering trough.

One morning, John came out to the kitchen in time to see a strange dog killing the second duck. "He is going for the third, Mom," he said. I ran out the door as fast as I could, picking up a stick along the way. The duck was heading for the pond. "Yes, quick, to the pond," I said. Before I could get there that big rascal of a dog jumped into the pond and caught the duck. I made him give up the duck.

I carried the duck to the house but it was too badly hurt to save. We had to kill him but I could not cook him. The ducks were my pets and I could not eat them. They were also too badly bruised. I felt angry at the dog. I understood it was a dog's way of life, but he took all three of my ducks at once without warning. I never got ducks again as I was afraid the dogs would kill them. Later I did get a goose. He was not meant to keep as a pet and we butchered him in the fall.

One day I went with Ira to Fredericksburg Stock Auction. He was raising veal calves and wanted to replace those he had sold. He took out all but the front seat of the station wagon and set up a sheet of two-foot high plywood behind the seat. Now the station wagon could haul six or seven calves. To my dismay he bought ten calves! That was really crowding it. On the way home they would shuffle around and loudly bleat for their mothers. I understood their need but did we have to have all this shuffling and noise?

The front seats were split seats. Suddenly they had a big ruckus going and were shuffling toward the front. One came leaping across the board right between us with his head, bleating with a very wet nose. I scooted to the dash of the car, but that didn't help much. Ira pushed him back, but they wanted to repeat the process. We had a flat tire and had to stop. Ira changed the tire and rearranged the calf situation. The rest of the three-hour drive home was a little better.

One by one the children left home, married, and started homes of their own in communities in other areas of Virginia, and in the states of Ohio, Pennsylvania, and Maryland. Later some of them moved back to the home area.

My Dad had a stroke that nearly took his life. He never completely recovered. His right side was paralyzed and he was unable to get up by himself. A lot of his time was spent in bed. After a few years he and Stepmother moved to my brother Enos' and his family. Dad had a lot of problems with fluid in his body. I went to see him during this time. His speech was still a little slurred. I had trouble understanding him at times.

Dad died in 1976, four years after his stroke. The fluid filling his lungs caused his death. He was 73 years old. Dad's body lay at my stepsister's house. We got there the night before the funeral. It was already dark and a blizzard was raging. There was a very long lane and two or three tractors were kept busy all night to keep the lane plowed and help the stranded cars get through. The temperature was around 12 below zero. The day of the funeral was clear and cold. Although it is always a time of grief and sadness when a loved one dies, I was truly glad for Dad's sake that he was finally at rest. Now he could be with his parents and with mother in Heaven. He had suffered much in his lifetime. Now he is free from it all. Dad loved the Lord and spending eternity with Him is the greatest joy a person can have.

With Dad's death, both my parents were gone. That is the way of life. The older generation goes on and the new ones come. I too am getting old. Ira and I became grandparents and then great-grandparents. I do not see my children, grandchildren and great-grandchildren as much as I would like, but I pray for them and thank God that they are all well and healthy.

EPILOGUE

It is now 2017 and I am living at the Stuarts Draft Retirement Community (SDRC) in Stuarts Draft, VA. I live alone in my apartment home. I don't feel alone as I have old and new friends in the other apartments and see them often in the public areas of the buildings.

We have many activities available to us here, including exercises three mornings a week. We have Saturday Night Live programs of music, singing or other entertainment. We have weekly Bible study, weekly prayer meeting and Sunday night Chapel.

We enjoy monthly tea parties. At these parties our chaplain dresses in character and gives a monologue of a well-known historical figure. I find history interesting, so I try to be there each time. We also take group trips and have other varied activities.

A few years ago we had an art exhibit open to the public. That same year two of my daughters, two granddaughters, and four of my great-grandchildren had exhibited our Four Generation Art Show at three different locations in Harrisonburg. The SDRC here gave a large portion of their exhibit space for our Four Generation Exhibit. We really appreciated the opportunity as it was a lot of fun for us all. Since I have been painting many years and have more time to paint, I had more paintings in the show and sold some. I continue to paint and sell some. I also paint to give as graduation and wedding gifts to my descendants. I am teaching a painting class here at the community.

My life is busy and full. I write for our "Village News". I have a patio with flowers, a Hummingbird feeder and other attractions for birds and squirrels. I enjoy feeding and watching them.

Many times I think back through my 90 years of life, with its happy and sad times. I see how God is always with me. The deaths of my parents, siblings, two husbands and my son, David, who died at age 50 in 1999 were difficult. I think no one can ever be prepared for a death in the family.

I also have happy memories as I think back to Ira and my early married years, the years of raising our family, and seeing them grow into responsible adults. Often Ira needed to be gone with his work into late evenings. Then we missed him, especially at supper, as that was often when we had fun as a family. I so much enjoyed the children when they were home. I continue to enjoy them, the grandchildren, and great-grandchildren.

REACHING OUT